GCSE
Rural Science 2

Bernard Salt

Head of Rural Studies,
King Edward VI School, Lichfield
Chief Examiner, Midland Examining Group

Cassell

CASSELL Publishers Limited
Artillery House,
Artillery Row,
London SW1P 1RT

© 1981, 1987 Cassell Publishers Limited

All rights reserved. No part of this publication may be reproduced, stored in a retrieval system, or transmitted in any form or by any means, electronic, mechanical, photocopying, recording or otherwise, without the prior permission in writing of the Publishers.

First published (as *Rural Science 3*) 1981
Second impression 1983
Third impression 1984

Second edition (as *GCSE Rural Science 2*) 1987

ISBN 0 304 313491

Design by Roger Walker
Line drawings by Oxford Illustrators Ltd

Typeset in Hong Kong by Best-set Typesetter Ltd.

Printed in Hong Kong by Wing King Tong Co Ltd

Cover photograph of a robin reproduced with the permission of Phillip Ward

Contents

	Preface	5
1	Botany	7
2	Herbicides	27
3	Protected cultivation	33
4	Fruit	62
5	Gardens	83
6	Sheep	98
7	Cattle	114
8	Intensive poultry production	141
	Answers to in-text questions	153
	Glossary	158
	Index	167

Acknowledgements

The author and publishers would like to thank the following sources who have kindly supplied illustrative material: Aberdeen Angus Society, British Friesian Cattle Society, J. W. Chafer Ltd, Douglas Low Photography, Farm Key Ltd, *Farmers Weekly, Farming Outlook* (Tyne Tees Television), Fordingbridge Engineering Ltd, J. R. Fullwood and Bland Ltd, Hereford Herdbook Society, and G. R. Hughes.

Preface

This book, together with *GCSE Rural Science 1* and *Start Rural Science*, covers the GCSE examinations in Rural Science set by the five Examining Boards.

It is based on Cassells' *Rural Science 3* and can be used to 'top-up' sets of these. There is additional material, however, particularly in Chapters 3, 4, and 5, and changes have been made throughout.

All the end of chapter questions are new and of a type likely to be used in GCSE examinations. In each case, however, Question 1 is a straight-forward comprehension question covering the whole chapter. Although each chapter is a complete unit in itself, the Rural Scientist is dictated to by the seasons and material can be used in any order.

My thanks to Mr W. Carnell for developing and printing the photographs.

Bernard Salt
Lichfield, 1987

1 Botany

Living things are made of small blocks called cells. The living material inside each cell is surrounded by a membrane and, in addition to this membrane, plant cells have a rigid wall. When a plant is cut the contents of any damaged cell spill out, but the walls remain intact. This can be seen with the aid of a microscope.

If plants are to be properly understood we must study the arrangement of the different types of cells within a plant.

Task 1.1

1. Cut a vertical slice from an onion.
2. Peel the fine inside skin from one segment.
3. Place a small piece of this skin on a microscope slide.
4. Add a drop of water and cover with a cover slip.
5. View under a microscope.

The pattern you see represents the thousands of cells from which the onion is made.

Are all the cells exactly the same size and shape?
...Q.1

All plants are made from tiny individual cells of living material separated by common walls of dead cellulose. Plant cells are not flat – as they may look under the microscope – but have three dimensions, like a cube:

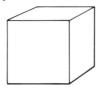

Inside the hard wall is a living membrane which contains living material – *protoplasm*. The centre of the cell is filled with a watery fluid – *cell sap*

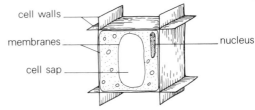

A stylised plant cell

The cell is blown up hard with water, rather like a bicycle tyre blown up with air. This keeps the cell rigid and gives the plant strength. The pressure inside the cell is known as *turgor pressure*. If there is not enough water to keep the cells turgid, the plant wilts.

A wilted plant (left), and (right) the same plant one hour after watering

If plant material is cut wafer thin and viewed through a microscope the cell structure can be seen clearly. Different types of cells within a plant perform different functions and look different under the microscope. These variations are easier to see when the section is stained with dyes. Specially prepared slides of stained plant material, cut one cell thick, are available for study.

The internal structure of the root

Task 1.2

1. View a prepared slide of a cross-section of a root. Look at the outside layer of cells and see how they differ from the ones immediately below. Look at the ring of cells around the central core: How many cells thick is this ring? How many different types of tissue can you see inside the inner ring? Which cells have thick walls and which have thin walls? (*Note:* a tissue is a group of similar cells performing the same function.)
2. View a prepared slide of the longitudinal section of a similar root. Note that the pattern you saw on the cross-section runs through the length of the root. Look at the length of the cells that form the tissue in the centre of the root.

Functions of root tissues

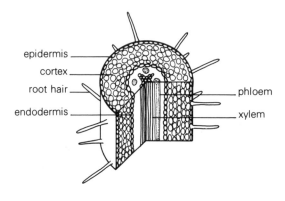

Epidermis
The outside skin that holds the root in shape, prevents loss of water and protects from bacteria and fungi.

Root hair
A single cell of the epidermis which grows in between soil particles. Root hairs stick to soil, helping to anchor the plant and prevent soil erosion. Root hairs have a large surface area which increases the ability of the root to absorb soil water.

Cortex
An area of food storage in loosely-packed cells with interconnecting air spaces.

Endodermis
A single layer of thick-walled cells which regulates the passage of water and mineral salts from the cortex to the stele (the area inside the endodermis).

Phloem
Bundles of fine tubes which transport substances that the plant has manufactured. For example, the phloem carries the materials for growth to the root tip, as well as substances to be stored in the cortex.

Xylem
Bundles of tough fine tubes with two functions:

(a) to transport water and mineral salts from the root;
(b) to give the root strength.

Although most of the features on the diagram will be clearly seen under the microscope, root hairs are often missing as they may be destroyed during the processing of the section for the slide.

Task 1.3

1. Soak five broad bean seeds for 24 hours.
2. Plant the soaked seeds in damp sawdust and leave in a warm room.
3. When the plumule is emerging, lift the seeds.
4. Gently shake off surplus sawdust and examine the root. Root hairs will easily be seen.

The internal structure of the stem

Task 1.4

Examine a prepared cross-section of herbaceous plant through a low power microscope. If the specimen is too large to allow viewing the whole at once, move the slide around to obtain an over-all view.

Using your knowledge of root structures try to recognise the different tissues, particularly the xylem and phloem which are grouped together in bundles (*vascular bundles*). Try to identify the thin layer of tissue between the xylem and phloem which is continuous from one vascular bundle to the next.

Functions of stem tissues

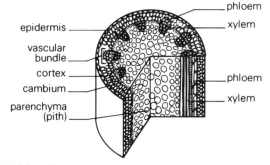

Epidermis
A single layer of uniform cells which form a tight skin around the stem. This skin keeps the cortex cells in position, prevents the loss of water and the entry of bacteria and fungi.

Cortex
Packing cells which help to maintain the shape of the stem. Air enters through *lenticels* (small holes in the epidermis) and circulates in the spaces between the cortex cells.

Vascular bundle
A bundle of xylem and phloem cells continuous with those in the root and performing the same function. It is important to remember that the phloem cells are on the outside of the bundle and the xylem cells are on the inside.

Cambium layer
The layer of cells where growth occurs. The cells of the cambium layer produce growth by dividing into two, each of which grows to full size and divides again.

Parenchyma (pith)
Packing cells. In some plants the parenchyma is absent and the stem is hollow, e.g. broad bean and parsley.

Comparison of the root and stem structure

An obvious difference between the root and the stem is the position of the vascular tissue – the strong part of the plant.

The stem is often subject to a sidewards stress, from wind and the weight of lateral shoots. The best structure to withstand this type of stress is a tube, and the vascular tissue in a stem forms a tube.

A root, being in the soil, does not usually have any sidewards stress. All the stresses in the root are along the length – a pulling force; the best structure to withstand this force is one in which strength is concentrated along the centre. The strongest tissue in the stem is tubular, like a lamp post, whilst the root has its strongest tissue down the centre, rather like a plastic-covered clothes line:

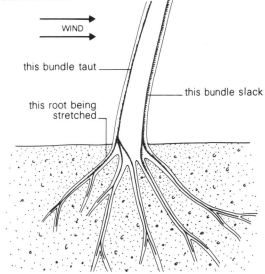

Stresses exerted on stem and root by the wind

The leaf

Task 1.5

1. Obtain a bottle of clear nail varnish or a bottle of the transparent fluid that typists use to correct stencils.
2. Remove a leaf from a broad bean plant (or other plant with a non-hairy leaf).
3. Paint the fluid on an area on the upper surface of the leaf about one centimetre square and a similar area on the lower surface.
4. When the fluid is dry, remove each square and mount on individual microscope slides.
5. Cover the squares with cover slips and view through the microscope.
6. The dry fluid will carry an impression of the surface of the leaf.
7. Draw diagrams showing the upper and lower surface of the leaf.

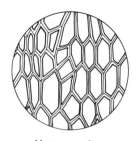 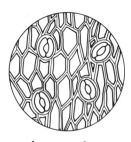

Upper surface   **Lower surface**

The upper surface of the leaf shows only the epidermal cells. The lower surface of the leaf shows the epidermal cells and also some pairs of sausage-shaped cells (see magnified views above).

The sausage-shaped cells on the lower surface of the leaf are called *guard cells* and the structure each pair forms is called a *stoma* (plural: *stomata*).

Task 1.6
Four experiments with leaves

Examine the four experiments described below, and decide what each experiment shows. Check your conclusions with those at the end of the book.

1. Two similar potted plants have polythene bags tied to seal the pots. One plant has its leaves removed and each plant is placed under a bell jar:

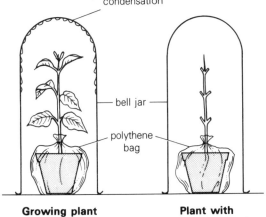

Growing plant   **Plant with leaves removed**

The four leaves are hung up and left. The control dries quickly and becomes limp, followed by the leaf with only its upper surface covered; the two remaining leaves become limp very slowly, perhaps taking several days.

3. A laurel leaf is cut and the cut end of its petiole sealed with petroleum jelly. The leaf is plunged into hot water and tiny air bubbles appear on its surfaces:

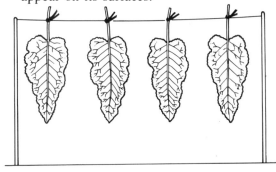

Control   **Vaseline upper surface only**   **Vaseline lower surface only**   **Coated with vaseline**

The jars are placed in a window and a few hours later the jar with the whole plant is clouded with condensation whilst the jar with the leafless plant is still clear.

2. Four fresh leaves are gathered. One is smeared all over with petroleum jelly, one has its upper surface covered with jelly, one has its lower surface covered with the jelly, and the last is kept clear as a control.

4. The leaf blade of a buttercup is placed under water and air is blown down the stalk. Bubbles are seen on the surface of the leaf:

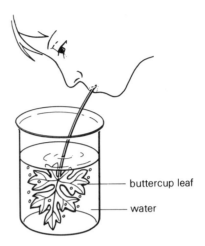

Stomata

Stomata are small holes in leaves which allow air and water vapour to pass through. Changes in environmental conditions cause changes in the turgor of the guard cells. An increase in turgor opens the pore and a decrease in turgor closes the pore; when a plant wilts, all the pores close.

Different plants have different numbers of stomata on their leaves – cacti have large numbers of stomata, and these can be seen easily if Task 1.5 is repeated using a cactus instead of a broad bean.

Investigation 1.1
To investigate the relationship between the number of pores and water loss

1. Obtain seven plastic petri dishes and a drill with a 1 mm bit.
2. Drill one hole in the lid of the first petri dish, two in the second, four in the third, nine in the fourth, sixteen in the fifth and twenty-five in the sixth.
3. In the seventh lid, drill as many holes as possible inside the 50 mm square, taking care that the holes do not join up.
4. Place the lids on the bases and carefully seal with sticky tape.
5. Use a hypodermic syringe to put 10 ml of water into each petri dish.
6. Leave on the laboratory bench to dry out.
7. Weigh each dish twice daily and record loss in weight.
8. Plot the results on a line graph using a different colour line for each dish (loss in weight on the vertical axis, time on the horizontal axis).

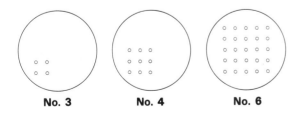

Drill the holes on a square pattern with 10 mm between each one and the next.

Functions of the leaf tissues

Cuticle
A layer of wax that prevents water loss, the cuticle covers all surfaces of leaf, petiole and stem except stomata and lenticels (pores in the stem).

Upper epidermis
The skin of the leaf, one cell thick.

Palisade layer
Vertical cells studded with chloroplasts (bodies within the cells which contain a green substance called chlorophyll). These move about in the cell as light intensity changes. It is inside the chloroplasts that photosynthesis takes place and sugars are manufactured from water and carbon dioxide.

Where does the water come from? ...Q.2
Where does the carbon dioxide come from? ...Q.3

Spongy tissue
Loosely packed cells with very large air spaces between, connected to the stomata so air can circulate freely within the leaf.

Task 1.7

Examine a prepared slide of a section of a leaf with a low power microscope. Identify all the parts shown on the diagram:

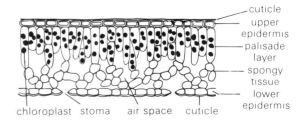

Internal structure of the petiole

Task 1.8

Take a leaf of plantain and gently pull the petiole in half; the tissue around the vascular bundles breaks and exposes them as in the photograph:

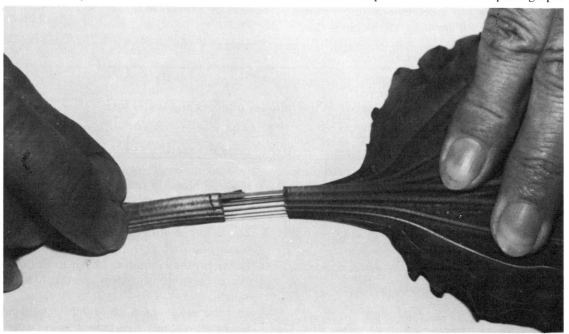

Take a single fibre and pull it upwards towards the back of the leaf; note how the fibre enters the leaf blade and begins to branch many times. Cut a cross-section of another petiole and examine it with the naked eye. Sketch a cross-section of the petiole.

Osmosis

Investigation 1.2

1. Remove the shells from two eggs simply by placing them in dilute hydrochloric acid and gently brushing them with a test tube brush.
2. Place one egg in a beaker of distilled water.
3. Place the other egg in a beaker of concentrated sugar solution.
4. Examine twenty-four hours later.

The egg in distilled water has swollen up.
The egg in the sugar solution has shrunk and become shrivelled.

The reason for the change in size of the eggs is water – either entering or leaving the eggs.

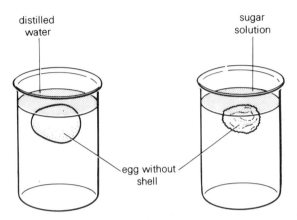

Which egg has water entered and which egg has water left? ...Q.4
How could water have entered the egg? ...Q.5

This investigation demonstrates a very important force in nature – osmotic pressure caused by *osmosis*.

Osmosis occurs when two solutions of different concentrations are separated by a semi-permeable membrane (allowing water through in one direction only). From Investigation 1.2 we found that the solution inside the egg had a different concentration from the solution outside and the membrane of the egg was semi-permeable.

In Investigation 1.2 did water move through the egg membrane from the strong to the weak solution or from the weak to the strong solution? ...Q.6

In osmosis water always moves from the weak to the strong solution. Plant membranes are also semi-permeable as the following experiment demonstrates.

Experiment 1.1

1. Peel a large potato.
2. Cut off one end to allow it to stand.
3. Scoop out a hollow in the other end as wide as possible and half the depth of the potato.
4. Put one teaspoonful of salt into the hollow and stand the potato in 25 mm of water.
5. Leave overnight:

The potato has acted as a semi-permeable membrane and osmosis has drawn water through the potato into the cavity.

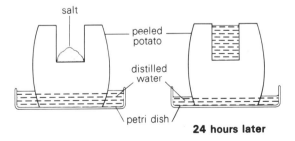

(*Note:* too much fertiliser will make a soil water solution more concentrated than the sap in the root hairs. This will result in water being drawn from the root by osmosis and the plant being killed.)

Transpiration

Water enters the root of the plant, travels up the stem and leaves as vapour through the stomata. This passage of water from soil to air through the plant is called *transpiration*:

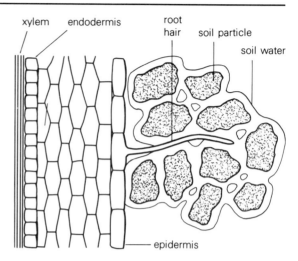

Root tissues through which water must pass to reach the xylem

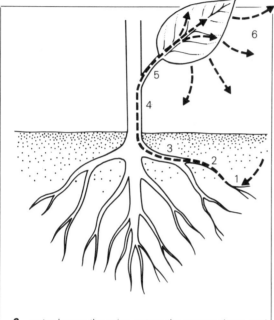

6. water leaves the veins, enters the spongy tissue and enters the atmosphere through stomata as vapour
5. water passes along petiole and enters the leaf veins
4. water rises up the main stem
3. water flows along the root
2. water passes into xylem
1. water enters the root hair

mis. This entry of water is important as it takes dissolved mineral salts to the endodermis. The endodermis 'pumps' water and mineral salts into the xylem vessels. Meanwhile, water evaporating from the leaves creates suction and water is drawn up the fine xylem tubes.

Investigation 1.3
To investigate the effects of different environmental conditions upon the rate of transpiration using a potometer

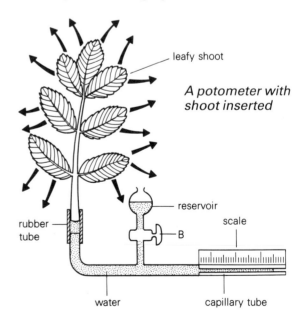

A potometer with shoot inserted

The transpiration stream

Soil water reaches the endodermis by two paths:

1. Soil water has a lower concentration than cell sap and enters the root hair by osmosis, the membrane around the protoplasm in the cell being semi-permeable. Inside the root hair the soil water reduces the concentration of the cell sap and passes to the next cell by osmosis. This process continues until water reaches the endodermis.
2. Soil water passes along the cell walls in between the cells until it reaches the endoder-

1. Cut a leafy shoot (large side shoot of tomato is ideal).
2. Submerge a potometer together with the cut end of the shoot in a bath of water. Cut 10 mm from the base of the shoot and fix it on to the potometer.
3. Remove from the water and dry with a paper towel.
4. As the tomato shoot transpires the miniscus at the end of the column of water moves along the capillary.
5. Using a stop-watch, record how long it takes for the miniscus to move along ten graduations.
6. Open tap B and return the miniscus to the end of the tube. Close the tap.
7. Repeat the timing along 10 graduations with the potometer in a number of environmental conditions: e.g., a humid greenhouse; bright sunlight; deep shade; forced draught, and so on. Record your results in each case.

Why was the same shoot used throughout the investigation? ...Q.7

Which condition would you expect to produce the most rapid transpiration rate, still air or a forced draught? ...Q.8

Plant growth

The growth of a plant is often observed by its increase in height:

An auxanometer

Small increases in height can be measured with an auxanometer, the pointer moving ten times as far as the plant grows. Each millimeter of plant height increase causes a movement of one division of the scale.

As the plant grows does the pointer move up or down? ...Q.9

Investigation 1.4
To investigate the effect of light on plant growth

1. Using an electronic balance, weigh 50 barley seeds together with three filter papers.
2. Place the filter papers in a petri dish and flood with water.
3. Arrange the barley seeds on top of the filter paper.
4. Cover with a polythene bag and seal:

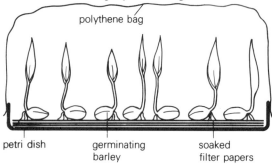

5. Obtain a second dish of seeds by repeating the above.
6. Place one petri dish in a window and the other in the dark.
7. Observe the dishes each day and water if required (the filter papers must not be allowed to dry out). Take care to reseal the bags.
8. When the barley growing in the light is about 100 mm high, remove the dishes from the bags and place them in an oven set at 110°C.
9. Leave for 48 hours, remove the dried up seedlings complete with filter paper and weigh.
10. Compare the weighings before and after sowing.

If the investigation was successful the plants growing in the dark will have lost weight and the plants growing in the light will have gained weight.

The plants grown in the light have increased their dry matter content and made *real* growth.

The plants grown in the dark have not increased their dry matter content; these plants have not made any real growth; the growth they did make was *apparent* growth.

Many plants grow without increasing in height, for example the carrot root may be growing rapidly whilst the parts above ground remain unchanged. The auxanometer only measures increase in height. The type of plant growth that is important to man is growth that increases the dry matter content (that is, plant weight excluding any water the plant contains).

All plants require light to make real growth.

Are dried peas soaking in water making real or apparent growth? ...Q.10
Is a bean seed germinating in the dark making real or apparent growth? ...Q.11
Is the increase in size of a carrot root (when the plant is in ideal growing conditions) real or apparent growth? ...Q.12
Is a potato tuber growing long shoots in a dark cupboard making real or apparent growth? ...Q.13

Plants make real growth in the presence of light by a process called *photosynthesis*.

Photosynthesis

Plants manufacture sugars from carbon dioxide and water. The energy for this process is obtained from sunlight, and some of this energy is locked up in the sugar molecule.

The plant process of building sugar from sunlight, carbon dioxide and water is known as photosynthesis:

$$\text{Carbon dioxide} + \text{water} + \text{sunlight} \longrightarrow \text{sugar} + \text{oxygen}$$
$$(CO_2) \quad (H_2O) \quad\quad\quad\quad (C_6H_{12}O_6) \quad (O_2)$$

Photosynthesis only takes place in the presence of a complex chemical called *chlorophyll*. Chlorophyll is the green pigment of plant leaves and stems.

A plant makes almost all its sugars in the leaf. Freshly made sugar is converted into starch and stored in the leaf, awaiting transport to other parts of the plant, where they are combined with mineral salts to make other materials, e.g. protein. The movement of substances through a plant is called *translocation*.

Botany 17

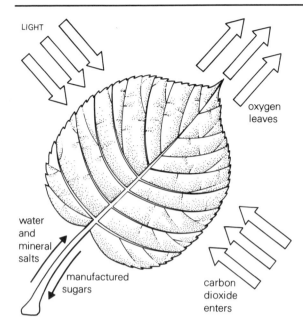

Exchange of photosynthetic materials in the leaf

Experiment 1.2
To test a leaf for the presence of starch

1. Remove a leaf from a plant and dip the leaf in boiling water for 30 seconds.
2. Using a water bath boil the leaf in methylated spirit until it has lost its green colour:

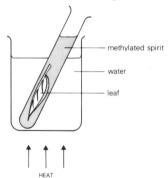

3. Dip the leaf once again into boiling water and place it on a white tile.
4. Paint iodine solution on the leaf. Parts which contain starch turn blue/black; parts which do not contain starch remain pale brown, iodine colour.

Experiment 1.3
To show that light is necessary for photosynthesis

Experiments 1.3–1.5 use a potted plant that has no starch in its leaves at the beginning of the experiment; this is achieved by keeping the plant in the dark for 24 hours prior to the experiment. The presence of starch in the leaf at the end of the experiment is taken as proof that photosynthesis has taken place (sugar minus water equals starch).

1. Exclude light from part of a leaf by pinning a piece of cork to either side:

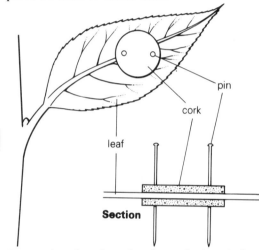

2. Leave the plant for a few hours in the window of a warm room.
3. Remove the leaf from the plant and the corks from the leaf.
4. Test the leaf for the presence of starch. Starch will be seen to be present in all uncovered parts of the leaf and in none of the covered parts, showing that light is necessary for photosynthesis:

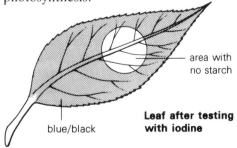

Experiment 1.4
To show that chlorophyll is necessary for photosynthesis

1. Use a plant with variegated leaves:
2. Place the plant in the window of a warm room for a few hours.
3. Remove a leaf and test for starch. Starch will be seen only in the areas of the leaf that were green. There will be no starch in the areas that were white, showing that chlorophyll is necessary for photosynthesis.

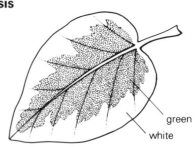

Experiment 1.5
To show that carbon dioxide is necessary for photosynthesis

1. Place two leaves in each flash as shown in the diagram.
2. Into one flash put a few pellets of potassium hydroxide (which absorbs the carbon dioxide from the air in the flash):

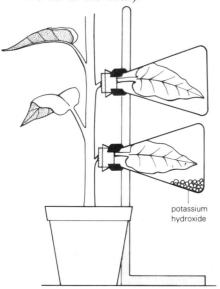

3. Leave the plant in the window of a warm room for a few hours.
4. Remove both leaves and test them for starch. Starch will be seen to be present in the control leaf but not in the one deprived of carbon dioxide.

Experiment 1.6
To show that oxygen is produced during photosynthesis

1. Set up the experiment as shown below with pond water and Canadian pondweed:

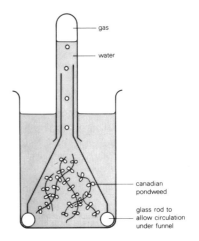

2. Place the apparatus in a window.
3. Set up a control experiment and place it in the dark.
4. When the test-tube in the light is about half full of gas (this may take a few days), test it with a glowing splint. The splint should relight, showing the gas in the tube to be richer in oxygen than the atmosphere.
5. Examine the control experiment; very little gas will have collected. This experiment shows that oxygen is produced during photosynthesis.

Factors affecting plant growth

All real growth in plants is a direct result of photosynthesis:

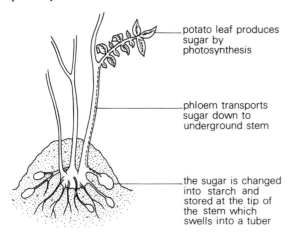

- potato leaf produces sugar by photosynthesis
- phloem transports sugar down to underground stem
- the sugar is changed into starch and stored at the tip of the stem which swells into a tuber

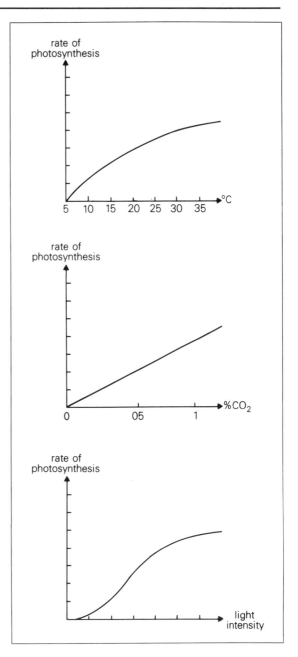

Conditions which favour photosynthesis will therefore also favour plant growth. The three graphs opposite show how the rate of photosynthesis varies with temperature, the amount of carbon dioxide in the atmosphere and intensity (brightness) of the light falling on the plant:

Study each graph and answer the following questions:

What was the rate of photosynthesis at 2°C? ...Q.14

Would an increase in the percentage CO_2 in the atmosphere increase or decrease the rate of plant growth? ...Q.15

What will be the effect on the photosynthetic rate if the temperature is raised from 30°C to 35°C? ...Q.16

What will be the effect on the rate of photosynthesis if the temperature is raised from 10°C to 20°C? ...Q.17

Does increasing light intensity increase or decrease the rate of photosynthesis? ...Q.18

There are other factors which affect plant growth, including: the length of the day; the availability of nutrients; the amount of water; the area of leaf; freedom from pests and diseases, and the concentration of carbon dioxide; this may be increased in a greenhouse – *carbon dioxide enrichment*.

Leaf area

Plants often have a larger area of leaf than the area of ground they occupy; the ratio of these two areas is called the *leaf area index*. The leaf area index of a plant is obtained from the following formula:

$$\frac{\text{area of plant leaf}}{\text{area of ground covered by plant}}$$

Task 1.9
To find the leaf area index of summer spinach

1. Sow a number of short rows of summer spinach 100 mm apart.
2. When the seedlings are large enough to handle, thin to 100 mm.
3. When the crop is covering the soil cut a plant of average size.
4. Remove all the leaves and spread them on 10 mm square graph paper.
5. Draw a pencil line around the outline of each leaf.
6. Obtain the area of each leaf by counting the squares. (Where the line crosses a square, estimate by discounting part squares smaller than half and counting part squares larger than half as one.)
7. Add the leaf areas together to obtain the total leaf area of the plant.
8. Calculate the leaf area index by dividing the total by 100 (the plant occupied 100 cm^2).

Beech leaves

Examine the photograph above and note how the leaves are arranged to obtain the maximum amount of light without shading other leaves. An important difference between wild and cultivated sugar beet is that the leaves of wild beet lie flat and tend to cover each other whilst the leaves of cultivated beet stand in vertical array, each receiving a good deal of light.

Leaf orientation

In addition to the area of leaf, the position of the leaf affects the amount of light it will receive; a leaf in shade will receive less light than an unshaded one. A leaf at right angles to incident light will receive more than a leaf that is not.

Investigation 1.5
To investigate the effect of leaf shape upon the rate of transpiration

There is a wide variety of leaf shapes. To discover whether the shape of the leaves has any effect upon transpiration rates, conduct the following investigation:

1. Cut from a piece of blotting paper a number of shapes that have similar areas, e.g.:

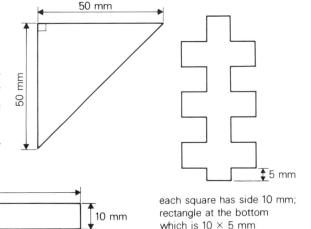

each square has side 10 mm; rectangle at the bottom which is 10 × 5 mm

2. Lightly smear the edges of the pieces with petroleum jelly to cancel the effect of the different shapes having different perimeters.
3. Use a graduated hypodermic syringe to moisten each shape with an equal volume of 15% cobalt chloride solution.
4. Hang the shapes to dry (cobalt chloride changes in colour from pink to blue as it dries).
5. Record the time each shape takes to change colour.
6. Draw conclusions from this investigation and check with those at the end of the book.

Suggest a method of conducting this experiment if no cobalt chloride solution was available.
...Q.19

Respiration in plants

A germinating seed, a growing root, a developing bud and many other plant processes will require some of the energy the plant has stored in sugars during photosynthesis.

The process of energy release from stored sugars is known as *respiration* and works upon the same principle as respiration in animals:

Sugar + oxygen ⟶ carbon dioxide + water
energy released

What gas is taken in by a respiring plant?...Q.20
What gas is released by a respiring plant?...Q.21

Plant nutrients

The water (H_2O) and carbon dioxide (CO_2) used by plants during photosynthesis supply only three elements: hydrogen (H), oxygen (O) and carbon (C). Plants require six other elements in fairly large quantities: nitrogen (N), phosphorus (phosphate) (P), potassium (potash) (K), calcium (Ca), magnesium (Mg) and sulphur (S). They require six more in very small quantities: iron (Fe), manganese (Mn), boron (B), copper (Cu), zinc (Zn) and molybdenum (Mo). As only a trace of the last six is required for healthy plant growth they are called *trace* elements.

The major elements (and one trace element) can be remembered by memorising the title:

C. Mg. HOPKONS CaFe

Substances which contain any of the essential elements, in a form which plants can absorb, are called plant nutrients. Although all plant nutrients are usually present in British soils three are often in short supply, namely nitrogen, phosphate and potash.

The addition of these three elements to the soil as fertilisers will almost always increase crop yield. It is important to remember that the chemicals contained in fertilisers occur naturally in the soil — fertiliser is added to increase the amounts available.

The three main elements can be supplied in either organic or inorganic form:

Element	Inorganic fertilisers	Organic fertilisers	Effect on plant
Nitrogen	Sulphate of ammonia Nitro chalk	Dried blood hoof and horn	Darker green leaves, more rapid growth
Phosphorus	Triple superphosphate Ammonium phosphate	Bone meal	Better root development
Potassium	Muriate of potash Nitrate of potash	Wood ash, kelp (the ash of seaweed)	Better flowers and fruit

Note: Nitrogen salts leach from the soil with the drainage water. These salts contaminate our drinking water and are a danger to health. Nitrogen fertiliser should be used very sparingly and only at times when crops are removing it from the soil (i.e. growing rapidly).

Fertilisers must always be applied according to the manufacturer's instructions and the recommended amounts never exceeded. For example, too much nitrogen makes the crop grow tall, weak and likely to fall, and can delay its maturity.

In practice crops usually require more than one nutrient and a range of products are available which contain all three nutrients – complete fertilisers.

The proportions of N, P and K in a complete fertiliser vary to meet the requirements of different soils and different crops. Proportions are shown on the container (usually a plastic bag) in the order N:P:K:

For example, this bag of fertiliser contains:
10 units of nitrogen,
5 units of phosphate,
12 units of potash.
The units are percentages – which makes calculations easy. For example, 100 kg of 12:12:18 will contain 12 kg of nitrogen, 12 kg of phosphate and 18 kg of potash.

How many kilograms of N, P and K will a 50 kg bag of 22:11:11 fertiliser contain? ...Q.22

These weights are important as fertiliser recommendations are given in kilograms per hectare (*note*: 1 kg per hectare = 0.1 g per m^2).

Fertilisers are supplied as small granules rather than powders because granules are easier to apply, they do not blow away and most break down slowly in the soil giving a continuous supply of their nutrients over a period of time.

Fertilisers are often incorporated in the seed bed but nitrogen leaches from the soil and some must be applied as a top dressing to the growing crop at the time when its uptake is likely to be rapid. Leached nitrogen fertiliser may enter a stream or river and have the effect of reducing the oxygen content of the water. This is caused by extra bacterial activity breaking down the additional plant material that the fertiliser encouraged grow.

All elements contained in the tissues of plants are cycled through nature:

the roots of a new plant absorb the element and the cycle begins again

the element is contained in the plant tissues

the animal dies and decays – the element enters the soil

an animal eats the plant and the element forms part of the animal

The nitrogen cycle

In practice natural cycles are much more complicated than this, as is seen in the nitrogen cycle.

Nitrogen is an essential part of protein, from which all living things are made. Although nitrogen is plentiful, forming 78% of the atmosphere, neither plant nor animal can obtain its nitrogen directly from this source. Plants absorb all their nitrogen through their roots as mineral salts. Animals obtain their nitrogen by eating food containing protein.

Nitrogen leaves the soil in the following ways:

Nitrogen enters the soil in the following ways:

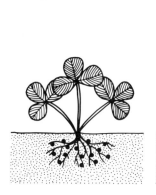

rhizobium bacteria in the root nodules of legumes use nitrogen in the soil air to make proteins

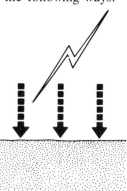

lightning causes atmospheric nitrogen and oxygen to combine—this dissolves in rainwater and is washed into the soil

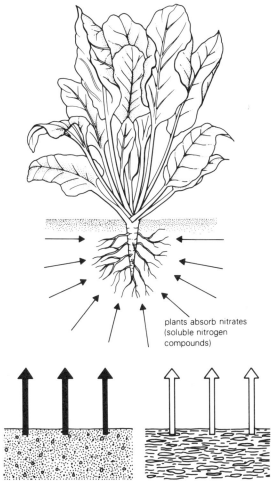

plants absorb nitrates (soluble nitrogen compounds)

farmers and growers add nitrogen fertilisers

de-nitrifying bacteria in the soil break down nitrogen salts, releasing nitrogen as a gas which enters the atmosphere

as organic matter decays, ammonia (NH_3) is produced which may be lost to the atmosphere

as the bodies of dead plants and animals decay, the protein they contain is changed into nitrogen salts by soil bacteria

animal faeces and urine are deposited in the soil; nitrogen contained in these is converted into nitrogen salts

Dead matter becomes nitrates in the following way:

action of various types of bacteria

These changes in the form of the element nitrogen can be linked together to form the *nitrogen cycle*:

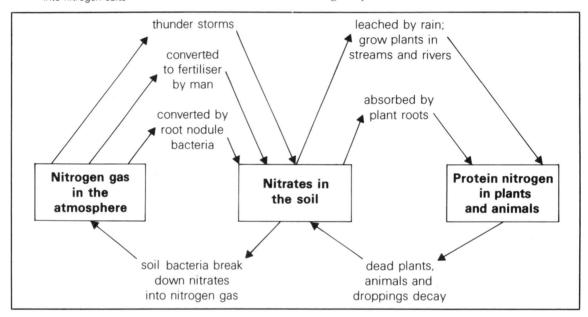

Task 1.10

1. Dig up a clover plant.
2. Gently shake all the soil from the roots.
3. Identify the root nodules and make a drawing of the root showing the nodules.

When legumes are ploughed into the soil, the nodules break down, increasing the amount of available nitrogen in the soil. Clover is often included in a ley, as it provides a source of nitrogen compounds, the bacteria in the root nodules fixing atmospheric nitrogen. Other legumes include peas, beans, lucerne, sainfoin, and lupins. The latter are sometimes grown and ploughed into the soil – a process known as 'green manuring'.

The carbon cycle

The element carbon is even more abundant in living things than nitrogen. Several atoms of carbon are present in every molecule of organic matter. During *photosynthesis* carbon is absorbed as inorganic carbon dioxide by plants and converted into organic material by combination with other compounds.

$$6\ CO_2 + 6\ H_2O \longrightarrow C_6H_{12}O_6 + 6\ O_2$$
carbon dioxide + water   glucose + oxygen

During respiration the carbon in the organic material is combined with oxygen, to form inorganic carbon dioxide which enters the atmosphere:

$$C_6H_{12}O_6 + 6\,O_2 \longrightarrow 6\,CO_2 + 6\,H_2O$$
glucose + oxygen → carbon dioxide + water

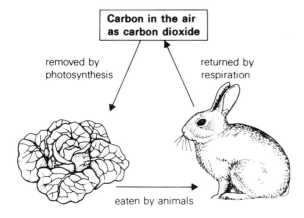

Task 1.11

Study the chart below and describe the three parts of the **carbon cycle** in full:

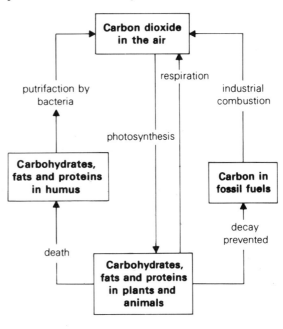

Questions: Botany

1. Write single sentences to answer the following questions:
   (a) How does the function of phloem differ from that of xylem?
   (b) Which gas is used up during photosynthesis?
   (c) Which gas is released during photosynthesis?
   (d) Which instrument is used to measure the rate of transpiration?
   (e) A shell-less egg placed in distilled water will swell up. What force causes this?
   (f) Which organism lives in the root nodules of legumes?
   (g) Which plant nutrient does 20:0:0 fertiliser contain?
   (h) What effect on the rate of photosynthesis does an increased concentration of carbon dioxide have?
   (i) What is meant by 'real growth' in plants?
   (j) Where is the starch which is stored in potato tubers manufactured?

2. Draw a cross-section through the stem of a dicotyledon.
   (a) Add the labels: epidermis, phloem, cambium, xylem, parenchyma.
   (b) What is the function of the cells in the cambium layer?
   (c) If bark is pulled from an actively growing tree it usually breaks from the main stem at the cambium, why?
   (d) Xylem and phloem are both conductive tissue, in what way does their function differ?
   (e) Why does the removal of a complete ring

of bark usually kill all the parts of a tree above the ring?

3. A bag of granular compound fertiliser has printed on it the following numbers:

   20:10:5

   (a) What do the three numbers mean?
   (b) The fertiliser could have been in powder form. What are the advantages of granules?
   (c) If the rate of application was 100 g/m² how much fertiliser would be required for a rectangular plot 50 m long and 12 m wide?
   (d) Name a crop for which this fertiliser would be
      (i) suitable.
      (ii) unsuitable.
      Give reasons for your answers.

4. (a) State three functions of roots.
   (b) Copy the diagram from page 14 which shows the internal root tissues. On your diagram, using two different colours, draw in the two pathways by which soil water reaches the xylem.
   (c) Describe the part played by the endodermis in the uptake of salts from soil to plant.
   (d) By reference to your diagram explain why too high a concentration of salts at a plant root will kill the plant.

5. (a) Design an experiment which would enable you to measure the amount of water transpired by a plant in one hour. Include at least one diagram and mention all the measurements you would take.
   (b) In what ways would your results be useful to a grower?

6. At a research station two greenhouses were set up to produce identical conditions, except that one had extra carbon dioxide in its atmosphere. Both greenhouses were cropped with lettuce for a whole year.

Results:

	Days taken for the crop to reach maturity	
Crop number	CO_2 enriched	Control
1	48	57
2	47	56
3	55	66
4	58	65
5	60	65
6	53	56
7	44	–
Total days	365	365

   (a) Suggest one method by which the carbon dioxide concentration in the atmosphere could be increased.
   (b) Why should the difference in the two atmospheres affect the growth of lettuce?
   (c) The lettuces in both greenhouses took longer to mature in winter. Why?
   (d) By reference to the table, state the main advantage of carbon dioxide enrichment for a lettuce grower.
   (e) If you repeated this experiment using tomatoes instead of lettuce, what differences would you expect to see between the two crops of tomatoes?

7. A dairy cow grazes a grass/clover mixture which receives a dressing of ammonium nitrate (manufactured from atmospheric nitrogen). The pasture is subject to the occasional thunderstorm.
   (a) Draw a diagram to show how the element nitrogen cycles through the atmosphere, soil, plant and cow.
   (b) By reference to your diagram show each point where microorganisms are responsible for the process.

2 Herbicides

Task 2.1

1. Dissolve 25 g of sodium chlorate in a litre of water (**caution**: sodium chlorate is inflammable, unless it contains a fire depressant), and water a small area of a weedy path with the solution.
2. Put a large pinch of sodium chlorate powder into the centre of a dandelion or thistle growing in a lawn.
3. One week later examine the path and the treated weeds. The weeds on the treated area of the path will be dead and so should the weed on the lawn. The bare patch on the lawn will become covered with grass as the sodium chlorate leaches out.

Sodium chlorate is a chemical substance that kills plants; such a substance is called a *herbicide*.

Sodium chlorate is sometimes used to kill the weeds growing in the bottom of an established hedge. If the correct amount of chemical is applied the weeds will be killed and the deeper rooted hedging plants will be unharmed (see diagram on right).

The sodium chlorate has been used in such a way as to kill the weeds and not the hedge. A chemical which can be made to work in this way is called a *selective herbicide*.

Earlier this century farmers used to spray their young cereal crops with a 10% solution of sulphuric acid. The broad, hairy leaves of many of the weeds held more acid than the narrow, upright leaves of the cereal plants. By carefully adjusting the amount of spray applied, the farmer killed many of the weeds without killing the crop.

What would be the effect of too much spray?
...Q.1
What would be the effect of too little spray?
...Q.2

In 1930 it was discovered that if plants were sprayed with paraffin or other mineral oil most were killed, but plants belonging to the family *umbelliferæ* suffered little and soon recovered. For many years after this discovery carrots and parsnips were kept weed-free by spraying with paraffin.

Which method of weed control favours the carrot fly: hand weeding or spraying? ...Q.3

These old (and often dangerous) methods are now little used as many new herbicides have been discovered.

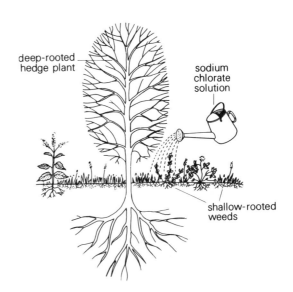

Modern herbicides

There are three main groups of herbicides:

1. Contact herbicides

These chemicals scorch any part of the plant they touch; those parts untouched are unharmed.

What effect will a contact herbicide have on: (a) a seedling; (b) an established perennial?

...Q.4

2. Translocated herbicides

This group of chemicals move inside the plant, disrupt its growth and cause its death. When spraying this type of chemical there is no need to cover the whole plant with spray as unsprayed parts will receive the poison by the plant's transport system. When sprayed on the leaves of perennials translocated herbicides move to the underground parts, killing the entire plant.

3. Residual herbicides

These chemicals are applied to the soil and taken up by plant roots. These chemicals often persist in the soil for several months.

Herbicides in common use include:

Contact	Translocated	Residual
paraquat	M C P A	simazine
diquat	mecoprop	propham
dinoseb	dichlorprop	diuron
ioxynil	glyphosphate	carbamate
	(tumbleweed)	

The same product is often sold under a number of different names, for example simazine is an active ingredient in all of the following: Boots Path Weed Control; GESAL Weedex; GESAL Specialist Weedex Mini-granules; Murphy Rose Bed Weedkiller; Murphy Simazine Total Weedkiller. Many brands of weedkiller contain two, or even three active ingredients in order to control a broad spectrum of weeds.

A A contact herbicide – paraquat

This herbicide destroys all the green tissue it touches. It is absorbed by the leaf and has the effect of destroying chlorophyll during photosynthesis, and, therefore, acts much more quickly in warm weather than in cold conditions. Paraquat is applied diluted in water in a fine spray to the leaves and is rendered harmless on touching the soil. A small amount of paraquat will kill a large number of plants: three litres, diluted with water, is enough to treat a hectare of weedy land. Plants absorb paraquat rapidly and a fall of rain soon after spraying does not wash it away. Paraquat is **extremely poisonous** so it is available (in concentrated form) only to farmers and growers. They have to sign a poison register when they make a purchase.

Paraquat is used in the following ways:

1. To kill all weeds around the base of fruit trees:

spray touches weeds only, not the trees

If soft fruit bushes (e.g. gooseberries and raspberries) are sprayed during the dormant period it does no harm as the buds are protected with scales. The buds of blackcurrants remain green and will be severely damaged if spray is allowed to come into contact with them.

2. As a pre-emergent spray. For example, a crop of carrots is sown and many weed seeds germinate before the carrots. Two days

before the carrots germinate the area is sprayed with paraquat, which kills all the weeds leaving the carrots to emerge in a weed-free bed (germination time is determined by sowing a few seeds two days before the crop is sown).

Pre-emergent spraying is commonly used for potatoes. The crop is sprayed when the shoots appear. The first shoots are killed along with the weeds, but the potatoes quickly produce new shoots and any weeds which germinate later die through lack of light.

3. Paraquat is used to kill unwanted foliage before harvest, such as the haulm of potatoes, which would clog the lifting machinery. Clover, grown for seed, is sprayed with paraquat before combining.

4. Paraquat is added to whitewash for marking out sports pitches. When the whitewash washes away, the dead grass shows the groundsman where to push the lining machine.

5. Cleaning stubble before direct drilling (on certain soils). After a crop of cereals has been harvested all weeds are killed with paraquat, the field is lightly harrowed and another crop of cereals sown – without the field having been ploughed. This is known as *direct drilling*, and it has the advantage of conserving moisture that would have been lost had the plough been used. Direct drilling has another advantage in that less energy is used for soil preparation.

B A translocated herbicide – MCPA

This is sprayed on the leaves where it does not cause scorching, but is translocated to all parts of the plant. Acting in a similar manner to auxins, MCPA disrupts the growth of the plant, causing stems and petioles to become elongated and distorted as shown in the photograph. The excessive growth weakens and kills the plant.

MCPA is very useful against deep rooted perennial weeds. Why? ...Q.5

A dock plant showing distorted growth five days after MCPA was applied

The effect of MCPA varies according to plant species. At low concentrations it has little effect on cereals and grasses but kills charlock, fathen, dock, thistle, hemp nettle, and many other weeds.

MCPA is used in the following ways:

1. To control many weeds in cereal crops.
2. As a lawn weed killer – MCPA kills dandelions, daisies and other broad-leaved weeds leaving the grass unaffected.
3. MCPA is used to kill persistent weeds under fruit trees, although care must be taken not to wet the soil. If the chemical is absorbed through its roots the tree will produce distorted shoots the following season.

C A residual herbicide – simazine

When simazine is applied to a weed-free soil it will kill many weed seeds as they germinate. Simazine will only work when the soil is moist and, in times of drought, the soil has to be irrigated before the chemical is applied. Simazine works much better in some soils than in others and the amount to be applied depends upon soil type and weather conditions. One kilogram of simazine, applied to one hectare, will remain effective for up to six months, although there are risks that resistant weeds will build up rapidly, e.g. knotgrass and cleavers.

What will be the effect of regular use of simazine in a field that contains many annual weeds and just a few knotgrass and cleavers? ...Q.6

Simazine is used in the following ways:

1. Immediately after drilling sweet corn and broad beans, simazine is applied to the surface, weed seeds present are killed as they germinate and the crop seeds are too deep to be affected.

What will be the likely effect of applying too much simazine? ...Q.7

2. Mixed with paraquat, simazine is used under fruit trees and over dormant gooseberry bushes; paraquat kills the weeds present and simazine has a residual effect in keeping the ground weed free for the following six months.

Why is this combined spray not used on dormant blackcurrant bushes? ...Q.8

3. Simazine is used to keep fallow areas free from annual weeds.
4. Simazine is applied to leeks (1.5 kg/ha) immediately after planting and keeps them weed free during their long growing season.

Susceptibility of some weeds to paraquat/MCPA/simazine

	Paraquat	MCPA	Simazine
Charlock	S	MS	S
Cleavers	MR	R	R
Chickweed	S	R	S
Couch	R	R	R
Fathen	S	S	S
Groundsel	S	R	S
Knotgrass	S	R	MR
Mayweed	S	R	S
Redshank	S	R	MS
Scarlet pimpernel	S	R	S
Shepherds purse	S	MS	R
Sow thistle	S	MS	S

Key: S = susceptible
MS = moderately susceptible
R = resistant
MR = moderately resistant

If the farmer has only the three chemicals shown in the chart then cleavers and couch would be most troublesome. Cereal growers are more dependent upon herbicides than other growers as they practise *monoculture* with as few break crops as possible. Weeds with similar characteristics to cereals are the most difficult to control, and include couch, blackgrass, and wild oats: herbicides which are effective against these also kill the crop. Couch can be controlled by treating in the winter with dalapon in between two cereal crops.

Machines to apply herbicides – sprayers

Most herbicides are dissolved in water and applied as a spray; the same type of machine is used to apply herbicides as is used to apply pesticides. The machine forces liquid under pressure towards a very small hole; the flow is interrupted before the hole is reached, breaking

A tractor-drawn sprayer

the liquid into small droplets, and the droplets emerge as a fine spray.

Tractor mounted sprayers are fitted with a pump driven by a p.t.o. and have many nozzles fitted along a wide boom. High volume sprayers deliver up to 1250 litres per hectare and low volume sprayers deliver 400 litres per hectare or less. Low volume sprayers are quicker to fill, reduce the need for water transport, are lighter to carry and cause less damage to the soil structure.

Translocated herbicides are usually applied by low volume sprayers as complete cover of the leaves is unnecessary for this type of herbicide.

Why is complete cover unnecessary? ...Q.9

A knapsack sprayer is useful where small areas of weeds are to be treated. The handle in the operator's right hand operates a pump which applies the necessary pressure to force the spray through the single nozzle.

The Health and Safety at Work Act has increased the regulations governing safety. It has made people more safety conscious. Chemicals

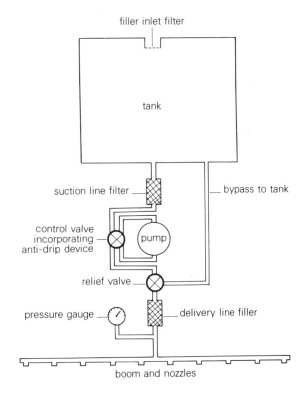

A hydraulic sprayer

may be carcinogenic (cancer causing), they may be toxic (poisonous), they may cause allergy or be harmful in other ways. Chemicals must be stored strictly according to the manufacturers' instructions and always locked in a secure place. Tractors being used to spray toxic chemicals must be fitted with a sealed cab and an air filtration unit through which the air enters. Excessive noise is dangerous to health; noise levels at a tractor driver's ear must not exceed 90 dB. Make sure that you do the Task below and compare your answer with the one on page 154.

Task 2.2

Herbicides and pesticides can be dangerous and must be handled with great care. Make a list of safety precautions that should be observed by anyone using these chemicals and compare it with the one at the end of the book.

In common with other agricultural chemicals herbicides can be extremely dangerous and all new products are tested by the Agricultural Chemicals Approval Scheme; tested products which are safe to use (providing the stated safety precautions are observed) are marked with this symbol:

AGRICULTURAL CHEMICALS APPROVAL SCHEME

Questions: Herbicides

1. Write single sentences to answer the following questions:
   (a) What is a herbicide?
   (b) How does the action of a contact herbicide differ from that of a translocated (systemic) one?
   (c) What mark appears on herbicides which have been approved by the Ministry of Agriculture?
   (d) Which herbicide destroys the underground parts of couch grass?
   (e) Why are potato tops destroyed with herbicide before the crop is lifted?

2. Herbicides can be extremely dangerous to health. List all the precautions which must be taken when handling and storing these chemicals.

3. In order to test a new herbicide a weedy arable area was harrowed in spring and left unsown. In early summer the vegetation was sampled just before the herbicide was applied. Further samples were taken the following day, two weeks later and six weeks later. The results were as follows:

Plant species	Number before application	Number one day later	Number two weeks later	Number six weeks later
Chickweed	480	510	10	300
Thistle	20	20	nil	5
Convolvulus	120	120	nil	nil
Dandelion	80	80	90	240
Mayweed	220	220	20	280
Fathen	170	170	70	190
Couch	50	50	nil	nil
Groundsel	300	320	30	230

(a) Draw two bar graphs, side by side, one showing the vegetation before spraying and the other showing the vegetation six weeks later.
(b) How can the apparent increase in chickweek and groundsel the day after spraying be accounted for?
(c) Suggest a possible reason why convolvulus and couch did not reappear. (They are perennials which produce rhizomes.)
(d) Which plant was resistant to the spray?
(e) Suggest reasons why some of the weeds recovered so quickly.

3 Protected cultivation

There are numerous structures of transparent material available to protect the growing plant from cold, wind, hail, rain and frost. The most common are:

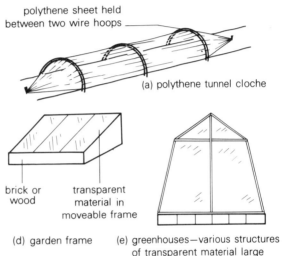

(a) polythene tunnel cloche — polythene sheet held between two wire hoops

(d) garden frame — brick or wood, transparent material in moveable frame

(e) greenhouses — various structures of transparent material large enough to walk inside

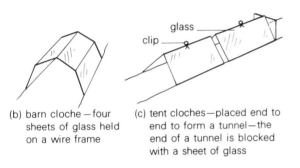

(b) barn cloche — four sheets of glass held on a wire frame

(c) tent cloches — placed end to end to form a tunnel — the end of a tunnel is blocked with a sheet of glass

Cloches

Cloches are usually unheated; in spite of this the temperature under cloches is often higher than the temperature outside for the following reasons:

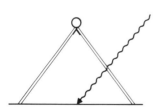

Day
Incoming radiation from the sun is in the form of short waves. Glass is transparent to short wave radiation which enters and warms the soil inside.

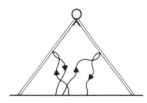

Night
At night the soil cools by long wave radiation, glass is opaque to long wave radiation which is reflected back, warming the soil.

This trapping of the sun's radiation is known as the 'greenhouse effect'. The greenhouse effect is not as apparent if polythene is used as this material is transparent to long wave and short wave radiation. Another disadvantage of polythene is that ultra-violet light destroys it and it has to be replaced every two years or so.

Experiment 3.1

Wet one thumb and blow upon both thumbs. The wet thumb becomes much cooler than the dry thumb because the water evaporating requires heat to turn it into water vapour; this heat (called latent heat) is removed from your wet thumb, thus making it cold.

Wind causes water to evaporate from moist soils, cooling them.

Wind does not dry soil under cloches which therefore will cool more slowly.

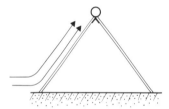

Soil is warmed by incoming radiation, the air is warmed from the soil. Uncovered soil has a high volume of air to warm and quickly loses heat.

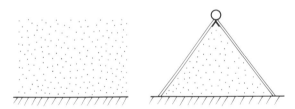

Warm soil under cloches has only a small volume of air to warm which takes only a little heat.

Name a crop pest which continuous cloches give protection from. ...Q.1

Cloches are not very tall – they are used to protect crops in the early stages of growth and are removed as the crop grows; by this time the weather is usually warmer. Examples of crops protected at this early stage include broad beans (variety Aquadulce), peas, cauliflowers, and maize.

Some crops can be left to mature under cloches, including anemones, daffodils, tulips (for cut flowers), lettuces, carrots and radishes.

Name another advantage of growing flowers under cloches in addition to producing an early crop. ...Q.2

In parts of the south-west large areas of strawberries are grown under cloches, some under polythene tunnels and some under the glass barn type. The root system of the strawberry is well established and extends towards the side of the cloche, obtaining water from the rainwater that is moving laterally in the soil, and the condensation that has run down the inside of the cloche.

The watering of small plants with restricted root systems presents difficulty under cloches – sometimes lengths of perforated hose are used, placed along the inside of the cloches; some cloches are designed to allow a pane of glass to be removed for watering, or the entire cloche can be moved.

The ploche (a small circular cloche) has a reservoir for water on top and eight small holes for the water to drip through – plants underneath can therefore be watered without removing the ploche. The photograph below shows ploches in a school garden covering germinating runner beans.

Task 3.1

1. Make a large copy of the following chart:

	Advantage	Disadvantage
Glass		
Polythene sheet		

2. Cloches are made from glass or polythene sheeting. Examine the list of advantages and disadvantages of these two materials and enter each in the approapriate box.

   Poor greenhouse effect; good greenhouse effect; easily broken; will not shatter; expensive; cheap; easy access; difficult access; lasts for many years; needs replacing every two years; light; heavy.
3. Check your answer with the answer at the end of the book.

Cloches have the following advantages:

1. They extend the growing season at either end.
2. They protect plants from late spring and early autumn frost, although on very cold nights the temperature under the cloche may fall below freezing point.
3. They aid crop succession.
4. They protect plants from wind, hail and rain damage.
5. They protect plants from birds.

Garden frame

The garden frame is a rectangular structure of brick, wood or metal covered with sloping, removable sheets of glass held in frames. Unlike cloches, frames are usually fixed and are not moved to the crop. Some frames have a soil base in which plants are grown, others have a gravel base and are used only for plants growing in pots or boxes. Some garden frames stand on rooting medium and are used for rooting cuttings.

Garden frames

As the garden frame is illuminated from the top only, it cannot be very tall or the plants inside would become etiolated.

Do etiolated plants have long or short internodes?
...Q.3

Although some garden frames have under-soil heating most are unheated and depend on solar radiation to maintain temperature. An unheated garden frame is called a *cold frame*.

A sudden change in the environment causes a reduction in the growth of plants and growers say such plants have been 'checked'. A badly checked plant will not reach its full potential and may even die:

The process of gradually acclimatising plants to outside conditions is known as 'hardening off'. It is most important that greenhouse plants are correctly hardened off before being planted outside.

Garden frames alongside a greenhouse – air is provided by removing one or more 'lights' (or frames)

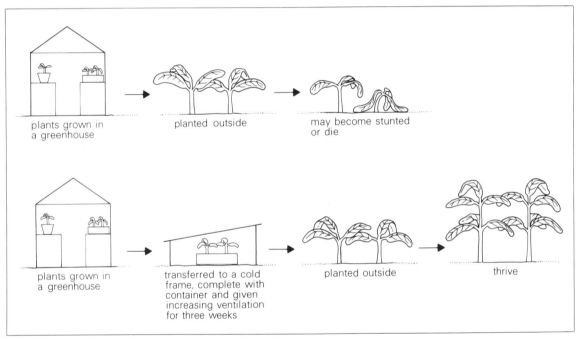

Greenhouses

The term greenhouse is used for any totally enclosed plant growing structure of transparent material in which the grower can walk upright.

Light enters a greenhouse in two ways:

1. Direct light from the sun which is received from one direction only.

2. Diffuse light which is received from all directions. Diffuse light is sunlight which has been scattered by water droplets and other agents in the atmosphere.

In Britain about half the light entering greenhouses is direct and half diffuse.

Materials for greenhouse construction

With the exception of a few expensive plastics, glass is the only suitable transparant material for a permanent greenhouse. The bars supporting glass sheets are called glazing bars and should be as thin as possible.

Why must glazing bars be thin? ...Q.4

Glazing bars are better spaced well apart – if bars are placed 600 mm (the most usual distance) apart, glass 3 mm thick will withstand all normal winds and snow loadings. If glazing bars are spaced 810 mm apart the thickness of the glass has to be increased to 4 mm to withstand normal stresses. The thicker glass transmits 2% less light and much of the advantage of having less glazing bars is lost.

Wood is a common material for glazing bars in greenhouses as it is somewhat cheaper than metal. The ideal material is strong, light, cheap and maintenance-free – aluminium has three of these four qualities, and in addition it is easily manufactured to the required shape and size.

Which three of the four qualities mentioned does aluminium have? ...Q.5

Steel is a good material for the main frame of a greenhouse as it has a low cost to strength ratio and is easily welded. Steel corrodes quickly and needs protecting by glavanising (coating with zinc) or painting.

Name two disadvantages of using wood for greenhouse construction. ...Q.6

The site

The site of the greenhouse should normally be level and free from shade.

The orientation will not affect the amount of diffuse light entering as this enters equally from all directions, but the amount of direct light entering the greenhouse is greater if it is sited from west to east instead of north to south.

Ventilation is necessary for the following reasons:

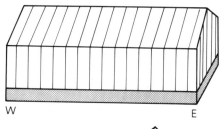
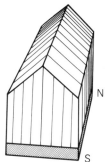

Orientation of greenhouses

a greenhouse orientated W–E admits more direct light than if it were orientated N–S

1. To prevent the air from becoming too warm during periods of bright sunshine.
2. To provide a constant supply of carbon dioxide for photosynthesis.
3. To reduce the humidity created by transpiration and evaporation.

Ventilators are situated at the top of the green-house and, in order to work correctly, most open an area equal to 15% of the floor area.

What size must the ventilators open to in a greenhouse 20 m wide and 100 m long? ...Q.7

The extent to which ventilators should be opened at any particular time depends upon windspeed, sunshine, temperature and the needs of the crop being grown.

Types of greenhouse

1. *Multiple span*

In addition to being multiple span this greenhouse is also mobile. Rails are fitted to the bottom of the greenhouse which run on the wheels seen in the foreground. When the top photograph (overleaf) was taken in April the greenhouse was full of tomatoes. The ground in front of the greenhouse is being prepared for late chrysanthemums, which will grow throughout the summer.

In October, when the tomatoes have finished, the whole greenhouse will be towed by tractor to cover the chrysanthemums which will flower during December and January.

The polythene tunnel consists of a metal frame over which a sheet of thin polythene is stretched. Crops inside can be grown directly in the soil, or they can be grown in boxes or growbags. The plastic sheet, however, is damaged by ultraviolet light from the sun and has to be replaced every three years. Although not as good as a glass structure it is very much cheaper and is widely used.

Protected cultivation 39

2. *Single span*

3. *Three-quarter span*

4. *Lean-to*

Which of the above types of greenhouse will admit most diffuse light (assume each covers the same area)? ...Q.8

Heating

An unheated greenhouse (a cold house) provides a sheltered and somewhat warmer environment for plant growth than outside, extending the growing season by up to four weeks at the beginning and a similar length of time at the end. To obtain extra benefits from a greenhouse it must be heated.

If a greenhouse is heated in winter to summer temperatures, will it provide an environment similar to that of summer? ...Q.9

To heat a small greenhouse throughout the winter is an extremely wasteful use of fossil fuels; the value of the energy used in often greater than the value of the plants in the greenhouse. Heating the school greenhouse during April and the first two weeks in May is beneficial and all that is necessary to grow the range of plants suggested in this chapter. (The heating period mentioned here is correct for the Midlands, but less heating will be required to the south and west, and more to the north and east).

There are two reasons for heating a greenhouse:

1. To raise the temperature of the air and soil.
2. To reduce the humidity as a high humidity encourages fungus diseases.

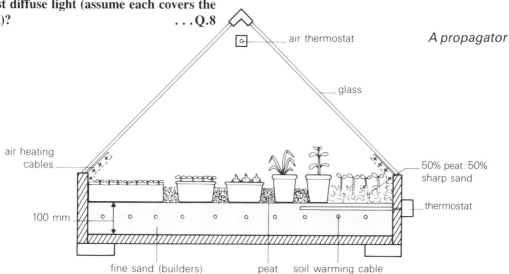

A propagator

Saving energy

1. Begonia, lobelia and other seeds with long germination times, requiring early sowing, can be placed in a large polythene bag and left in the classroom until the first cotyledons appear.
2. Early chrysanthemum cuttings and the first seed sowings are placed in a heated propagating frame inside the unheated greenhouse.

A soil temperature of 10°C will germinate brassica seeds; for most vegetables and flower seeds a soil temperature of 20°C gives rapid germination. 25°C is the best soil temperature for chrysanthemum cuttings.

Soil warming cable within the propagator is arranged thus:

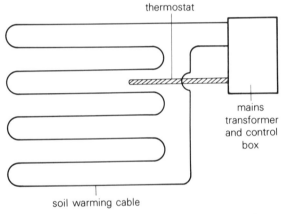

For safety, many schools insist on low voltage soil warming cables – these are thick and rather difficult to lay. The low voltage is obtained by using a transformer connected to the mains, reducing the 240 volts to either 6 or 12 volts.

A good mains cable is available for heating propagating frame soils. This cable is connected at one end only; it has the advantage of being thin and flexible, also no transformer is required.

The mains heating cable is protected by an earthed screen which makes it safe to use:

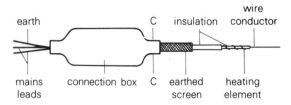

To complete the circuit, the wire conductor and the heating element are connected at the end of the cable.

Task 3.2

Draw a cross section of the screened heating element through C – C and check your drawing with the one at the end of the book.

Note: although the propagating frame described is easily made by an amateur, all electrical wiring must be carried out by an electrician, and the work approved by the National Inspection Council for Electrical Installation Contracting.

Soils and growing media in greenhouses

Glasshouse owners usually grow the same type of crop each year and, as the houses are static, crop rotation is not possible. Under these conditions the soil deteriorates and pests and diseases build up. One method of dealing with this problem is to partially sterilise the soil with heat or chemicals.

Heat sterilisation

The effect of temperature on soil organisms

Temperature (°C)	Organisms killed
55	Macro-organisms; earthworms; eelworms; seeds; viruses; some fungi; bacteria which convert ammonia into nitrates.
100	Other fungi; bacteria which convert organic matter into ammonia (these bacteria produce spores which can withstand this high temperature).
125	All living organisms are killed.

The coversion of organic matter into nitrates is a two stage process involving two different types of bacteria:

A quantity of soil is heated to 95°C. How would this affect the amount of ammonia present?
...Q.10

There are many methods of sterilising soil available to the commercial grower, including steam ploughs – which inject steam into the soil as they are slowly pulled along – and propane heaters – in which the soil falls down a rotating drum around a propane flame.

Chemical sterilisation
Soil may be sterilised chemically by the following method:

1. One litre of 40% formaldehyde is diluted 45 times.
2. A layer of soil 150 mm deep is spread onto a concrete floor.
3. The formaldehyde is applied to the soil with a watering can until it is soaked.
4. A second layer is put on top and treated in the same way and so on.
5. The heap is built up in layers until it is about one metre high.
6. The heap is covered with wet sacks and left for 48 hours.
7. The sacks are removed and the heap turned to allow the formaldehyde to escape.
8. Five weeks later the soil is ready to use.

Note: it is no use sterilising soil and then using it in dirty pots and boxes – strict hygiene must be observed. If soil is to be mixed on the floor then the floor should be sterilised with formalin (2%) beforehand.

Sterilising soil is expensive. So growers have developed several ways of producing crops with little or no soil – see the section on tomatoes. All of the recipes which follow specify the use of sterilised loam, but perfectly good composts can be made with unsterilised loam, providing there are not too many weed seeds present.

Garden soil is unsuitable for growing plants in pots and boxes for the following reasons:

1. Small quantities of garden soil dry out quickly.
2. Small quantities of garden soil packed into pots do not have enough pores for good root development, good air content or good drainage.

Experiment 3.2

1. Obtain an old saucepan with a capacity of at least 4 litres.
2. Pour in water to a depth of 30 mm.
3. Take a seed tray and fill it with top soil, taking care not to include any earthworms, and tip it into the saucepan.
4. Heat the saucepan until steam is rising freely through the soil.
5. Continue heating for five more minutes.
6. Allow the soil to cool.
7. Tip the soil into a *clean* seed tray.
8. Fill a second seed tray with unheated top soil.
9. Water both trays, place in a large transparent plastic bag and leave in the window.
10. Inspect the trays weekly for the next four weeks and record your observations.

Composts

Plants in pots and boxes are grown in mediums called 'composts'; this word should not be confused with the compost of the compost heap. John Innes composts were developed many years ago and are still widely used. They are mixtures of loam, peat and coarse sand with added nutrients.

The ingredients

1. *Loam*
This is produced by stacking turf upside-down and leaving for one year. The turf for loam making should be carefully selected. It should not have too many perennial weeds in it nor should it be either too sandy or too clayey.

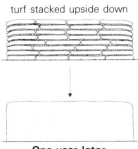

turf stacked upside down

One year later
the turf has rotted and the stack appears exactly like a stack of topsoil

Preparing loam

Before use loam is passed through a coarse garden riddle.

2. *Peat*

Peat is partially rotted plant material that has been cut from peat bogs and dried. If peat is very dry it should be wetted before use.

3. *Sand*

Sand must be coarse with no fine material in it. On no account should builders' sand be used as this can be too fine.

4. *Chalk*

A small quantity of finely-ground chalk may be necessary to adjust the pH to 6.5.

5. *John Innes base*

The base provides the essential nutrients N, P and K.

It is a mixture of: Two parts by weight of hoof and horn to supply nitrogen (slowly released as bacteria break the material down); two parts by weight of superphosphate to supply phosphate; one part by weight of sulphate of potash to supply potash.

The other necessary nutrients and trace elements are provided by the loam.

Peat provides the extra water holding capacity.

Coarse sand assists drainage and helps provide additional air space. An alternative to John Innes base is a product called 'Vitax'; it is added to composts in the same quantities as J.I. base, and has the advantage that its nutrients are available over a longer period.

Analysis of 'Vitax': nitrogen 5.3%, phosphate 7.5%, potash 10%, magnesium 1.75%, iron 0.25%, plus a trace of manganese, copper, boron and molybdenum.

Making John Innes compost

John Innes composts must be mixed on a clean site and a concrete floor that has been chemically sterilised is ideal. A volume measure is required – a ten litre box (such as that shown in the photograph) is suitable for class use:

1. Measure the amount of loam required and spread it on the floor to a depth of 150 mm.
2. Measure the peat and spread it evenly over the loam.

Mixing compost using a 10 litre box (internal dimensions 20 cm × 50 cm × 10 cm)

3. Measure the coarse sand and spread it evenly over the peat.
4. Weigh the John Innes base and sprinkle it carefully over the sand to obtain an even distribution
5. Using a clean spade turn the heap into a pile on one side.
6. Turn the pile back again.
7. Turn a third time and the compost is ready for use.

Recipe for John Innes seed compost
(Used for germinating seeds)

2 parts loam	1 g/litre superphosphate
1 part peat	½ g/litre chalk
1 part coarse sand	(if required)

How do you known whether the chalk is required? ...Q.11

Receipe for John Innes potting composts
(Used to grow plants in pots and boxes)

7 parts loam	2 parts sand
3 part peat	½ gram per litre chalk
	(if required)

To this mixture is added

3 grams per litre base fertiliser for J.I. No. 1 compost
6 grams per litre base fertiliser for J.I. No. 2 compost
9 grams per litre base fertiliser for J.I. No. 3 compost.

J.I. No. 1 compost is used for pricking out delicate seedlings.
J.I. No. 2 compost is a general purpose compost.
J.I. No. 3 compost is used for plants that require large amounts of nutrients, e.g. tomatoes.

If one plant tray takes three litres of compost to fill it, how many plant trays will a single mix of J.I. potting compost fill if a ten litre box was used to measure the ingredients? ...Q.12

How many two litre seed trays will a single mix of seed compost fill if a ten litre box was used to measure the ingredients? ...Q.13

'No soil' composts

Good loam is difficult to obtain; it is also heavy and expensive to transport. But you can buy a number of composts made from peat or peat and sand, enriched with nutrients and trace elements. 'No soil' composts are light, easy to handle and grow good plants.

A greater degree of skill is required when watering, as 'no soil' composts can become waterlogged, or so dry they will not wet. However, the main reasons why the author does not recommend their use are that they are expensive and that pupils using them lose the pleasure and experience of preparing their own.

Project 3.1
To grow a number of boxes of bedding plants

Bedding plants are half-hardy annuals, raised in greenhouses and planted into flower borders when the danger of late spring frost has passed. A half-hardy plant is one that flourishes outside in the summer, but is killed by spring or autumn frosts.

What is an annual? ...Q.14

Part A Preparing the seed compost

1. Using a 75 mm plant pot as a measure, put six measures of loam, three measures of peat and three measures of coarse sand on a bench, in a single pile.
2. Weigh three grams of superphosphate and sprinkle it over the pile as evenly as possible.
3. Thoroughly mix the compost, crushing any lumps between the fingers and thumb.

Part B Sowing the seeds

1. Take a clean seed box and place it on the bench by the pile of compost. The seed box needs to be at least 50 mm deep.
2. Pile all the compost in the box making sure the corners are well filled (see over).

3. Remove the excess compost by pushing a board across the top:

4. Take a packet of seeds, empty the contents on a card and sprinkle them evenly and thinly on to the compost; return any unused seeds to the packet.

Seeds in the following list are satisfactory: mesembreanthemum, petunia, nemesia, allysum, tagetes, French marigold, African marigold, aster, stocks, ageratum.

There are many other types of bedding plants, but this list is the most suitable for school use. If sown at the end of the spring term they are ready for pricking out during the first week or so of the summer term and are nicely hardened off by the beginning of June (Midlands).

5. Carefully sprinkle a thin layer of compost over the seeds. If a fine riddle is available it can be used to apply this covering but care must be taken not to bury some seeds much deeper than others.
6. Firm with a fitting board, pressing the compost 5 to 10 mm below the lip of the box:

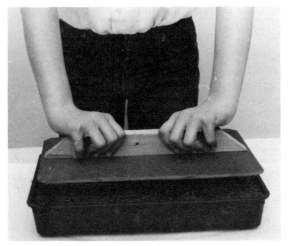

7. Using a fine rose thoroughly water the compost:

8. Write a label in pencil or waterproof ink; write the variety and the date of sowing, beginning at the square end; leave the point clear in order that the words are not hidden when the point is in the soil:

    TAGETES   Fiesta
    31 March

Do not thrust the label into the compost but insert it between the box and the compost.

Protected cultivation 45

9. Place the box in a greenhouse and cover with black polythene.
10. Examine every day and remove the polythene as soon as the first signs of germination are observed.
11. Water when required with a fine rose watering can; give a good soaking and do not water again until the compost begins to look dry. Water should not be taken from the cold tap but from a tank which is kept filled in the greenhouse.

Why not take water from the tap? ...Q.15

Part C   Pricking out

1. As soon as the seedlings are large enough to handle, using a 75 mm plant pot as a measure, put seven measures of loam, three of peat and two of coarse sand on the bench in a single heap. Sprinkle 18 g of John Innes base evenly over the heap and mix thoroughly.

This mix is approximately three litres. What type of compost have you just prepared? ...Q.16

2. Fill a plant tray with the newly-mixed compost in the same way as described in part B of this project. It is important to fill the tray correctly; a half-filled tray will not provide sufficient moisture and nutrients for plant growth nor room for good root development.
3. Firm the compost with a board pressing it about 10 mm below the edge of the box.
4. Dig up a small clump of seedlings from the box with a pointed stick or wooden label:

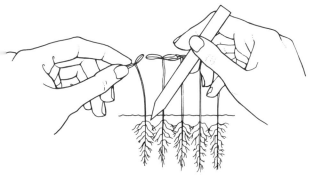

5. Take a single seedling by its leaf and, using the label, gently tease it away from the others retaining as much of the root and attached compost as possible.

NEVER HANDLE A SEEDLING BY ITS STEM—TOUCH ONLY THE SEED LEAF.

What is another name for a seed leaf? ...Q.17

6. Make a hole in one corner of the box of the potting compost about 30 mm from the side and the end.
7. Lower the seedling into the hole:

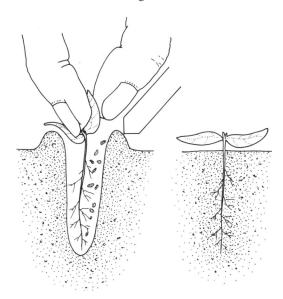

8. Make sure the seedling is as deep as, or a little deeper than, it was in the seed tray and fill in the hole with compost.
9. Plant five more seedlings across the end of the box to give a row of six evenly spaced plants:

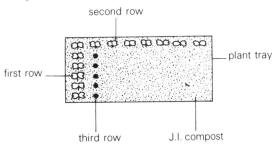

10. Complete a row down the side of the box by planting seven more seedlings, carefully and evenly spaced.
11. Complete the rows across, giving a box of 48 plants.
12. *Gently* carry the box to the greenhouse and place on the staging.
13. Water with a rose can.
14. Grow on in the greenhouse for three or four weeks.
15. Harden off in a cold frame as described on page 36.

The most common errors pupils make when growing bedding plants are:

 *Insufficient compost is placed in the seed box and plant box.
 *Seeds are sown too thickly.
 *Seedlings are handled by the stem.
 *Seedlings are planted in twos and threes instead of singly when pricking out.
 *Seedlings are disturbed after pricking out by too rough handling of boxes.
 *Incorrect watering.

The first five errors are easily avoided by care and attention to detail. The correct watering of plants in a greenhouse is much more difficult to learn; always give a good soaking, using a rose can, with water at greenhouse temperature, do not water again until the compost is looking dry. After watering the plants, thoroughly wet the floor of the greenhouse; this is known as 'damping down'.

How does wetting the greenhouse floor affect the plants? ...Q.18

Seedlings before (left) and after (right) pricking out

Tomato (*Lycopersicon esculentum*)

The tomato grows wild in the Andes mountains of South America; it was introduced to Europe, through Italy, in the sixteenth century and has become the most widely-grown greenhouse crop in Britain. The tomato plant is a herbaceous perennial but is grown as an annual.

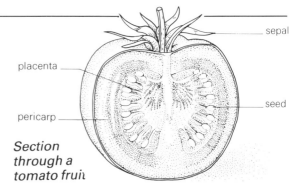

Section through a tomato fruit

Protected cultivation **47**

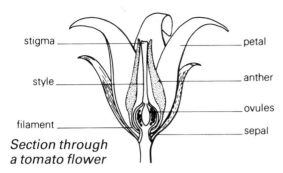

Section through a tomato flower

The tomato fruit is rich in vitamins A and C and is good to eat, yet the green parts of the plant contain poisonous chemicals and must not be eaten or fed to livestock.

Project 3.2
To produce good tomato plants

If a heated greenhouse is not available this project can be carried out in the classroom. Etiolation can be prevented by placing the plants in a window and erecting aluminium foil behind to reflect light back onto the plans:

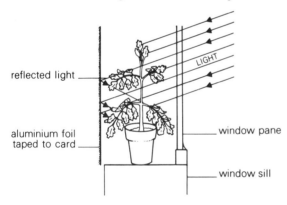

If an unheated greenhouse is available begin the project in the classroom and transfer to the greenhouse when the night temperature remains above 12°C.

What instrument would you use to check the lowest night temperature?   ...**Q.19**

1. Purchase a packet of tomato seeds (Moneymaker, Eurocross, or a similar indoor variety).
2. Sow the seeds thinly in a box of J.I. seed compost.

3. As soon as the seedlings are large enough to handle, prick out into 75 mm pots of J.I. No. 2 potting compost, one seedling in each pot – this is known as 'potting up':

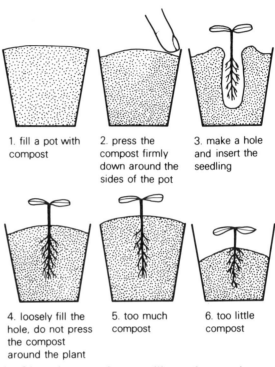

4. Give the growing seedlings the maximum amount of available light. Water as required.
5. Two or three weeks later, turn a plant upside down, tap and remove the pot. If the roots have reached the sides and bottom of the soilball proceed to 6, below.
6. (a) Take a 125 mm pot, put No. 3 potting compost into the bottom and firm gently.
   (b) Place a tomato plant in the centre, taking care not to disturb the ball of soil:

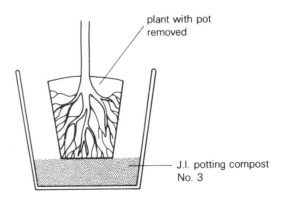

(c) Put compost around the outside of the ball, a layer at a time, firming each layer with the thumbs. Continue until the pot is filled; on no account must pressure be applied to the top of the soil ball or the roots will be damaged.
7. After repotting the plants (known as 'potting on'), return them to the greenhouse or classroom window.

A few weeks later the compost in the 125 mm pots will be full of roots and the tomato plants will be ready for moving to their final positions.

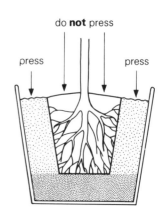

Project 3.3
To grow tomatoes by four different methods

A greenhouse is ideal for this project, but if a greenhouse is not available it may be possible to use the area against a south facing wall. In colder areas the 'grow-bag' method can be used inside, against a large window.

Work common to all four methods:

Support
Tomatoes have very weak stems and require support.

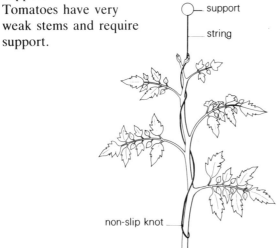

Either tie a length of tomato twine loosely around the base of the plant (above), twist the twine once or twice around the stem and fix it to a firm support immediately above the plant. As the plant grows the top is twisted around the string now and again.

Or push a garden cane upright into the soil alongside the stem, no further than 50 mm from the base. Tie the plant stem loosely to the cane with raffia at 250 mm intervals. The longer the cane the better but the actual length of cane will depend upon the amount of headroom available. This method is not suitable for grow-bags:

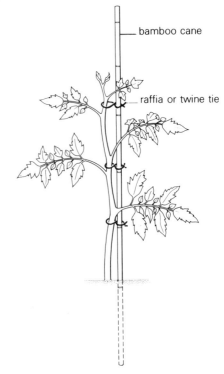

Side shoots

Once the plants are growing vigorously remove the lateral shoots as they appear in the leaf axils at the nodes:

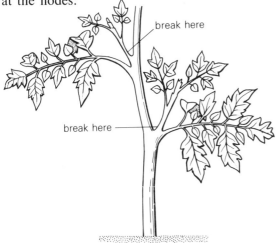

This will help the plants grow tall and make the maximum use of the space available in the house.

Lower leaves

When the tomatoes on the bottom trusses begin to change colour remove the lower leaves with a sharp knife to allow light and air to reach the ripening fruit. The additional air circulation helps to prevent fungus diseases developing.

Watering

Keep the growing medium wet but not waterlogged. In dull weather no water may be required on some days, but during sunny weather, when transpiration rates are high, water may be required every day. While watering, direct a jet of water directly into the flowers, as this assists pollination and fertilisation.

What is the result if the flowers fail to set? . . . Q.20

Always damp the floor of the greenhouse first thing in the morning.

Ventilation

Open the ventilators in the ridge of the house each morning and close them before going home. On cold days (below 17°C) leave the ventilators closed.

Method 1   In the soil bed

1. Remove the soil from a bed in the greenhouse to a depth of 600 mm.
2. Replace the soil with a mixture of equal quantities of topsoil and well-prepared material from the compost heap.
3. Allow the bed to settle for about three weeks.
4. Dig a hole in the bed large enough to take a 125 mm pot. Tap a plant from its pot and place it in the hole; firm the soil around the plant taking care not to disturb the soil ball.
5. Plant the other plants in a row allowing 400 mm between them.
6. Water, ventilate and support the plants as described above.

Method 2   The straw bale

1. Purchase a bale of straw (approx. 25 kg) and place it on the greenhouse floor.
2. About three weeks before the tomato plants are ready, thoroughly soak the straw with water, and water it daily afterwards. Bales of straw often heat up when they are first wetted, to a temperature high enough to damage plant roots.
3. Make two holes in the top of the bale with a sharp knife, each large enough to take a 125 mm pot.
4. Remove the pots from two tomato plants and place one in each hole:

5. Grow the plants as described, removing side shoots, supporting and watering.

6. Buy some fertiliser suitable for tomatoes and, after the first fruit has set, feed the tomatoes according to the manufacturer's instructions. This involves adding a measured quantity of fertiliser to the water in the watering can each week.

What causes the straw to heat up when it is first wetted? ...Q.21

A useful experiment is to use two straw bales. Feed the tomatoes in one bale and leave the second without feed. The effects of nutrient deficiency can be observed.

Method 3 Grow-bags

Grow-bags can be made up from old fertiliser bags, peat and 'Vitax' but for the purpose of this experiment a purchased one is recommended.

1. Purchase a grow-bag.
2. Place it in the greenhouse, either on the staging or on the floor, where supporting strings can be attached.
3. Cut two holes, 300 mm square, in the top of the grow-bag.
4. Carefully pour ten litres of water into the bag.
5. Make two holes in the peat large enough to take a 125 mm pot.
6. Remove two tomato plants from their pots and 'sit' them in the holes.
7. Support the plants, water, ventilate and remove side shoots as described above.
8. When the first fruit is formed feed regularly with purchased liquid tomato fertiliser in accordance with the manufacturer's instructions.

Method 4 Ring culture

1. Remove the soil from a bed, or use a large wooden box.
2. Fill the hole (or box) with either coarse sand or coal ashes.
3. On top of the sand place a 'whale hide ring' (this is a 225 mm diameter ring of felt material about the same height as a plant pot of that diameter). Empty plastic containers with tops and bottoms cut off may be used instead.
4. Put some John Innes No. 3 potting compost in the bottom of the ring and firm.
5. Remove a tomato plant from its pot and plant it in the ring, packing the compost firmly around the soil ball without disturbing it.
6. Make sure that 25 mm of ring remains above the compost to facilitate watering. Plant more rings in the same way, allowing 400 mm between plants.

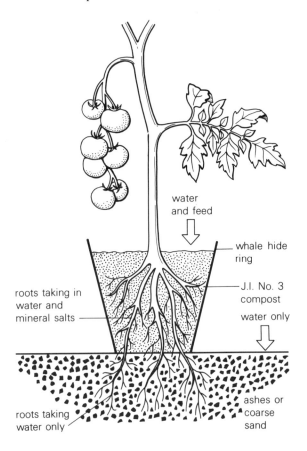

7. Water, ventilate, support and remove side shoots as described. In addition to watering the compost in the ring soak the sand daily.
8. After the first fruit has set, feed the plants with liquid tomato fertiliser on top of the compost only. Do not water the sand with water containing fertiliser as it will drain away and be wasted.

In addition to waste, what other reason is there for not watering the sand with fertiliser? ...Q.22

Methods 2, 3 and 4 above all use little or no soil; as crop rotation is not possible in greenhouses, soils quickly become infested with pests – especially eelworm – and must be sterilised or replaced. Soil sterilisation is expensive and growers have tried many methods of growing tomatoes, and other greenhouse crops, with little or no soil.

The tomatoes in the photograph are growing in black polythene channels along which is circulating water containing nutrients; the roots are bathed in this solution and there is no soil at all. This method of culture is known as *hydroponics* or *nutrient film technique* and is widely practised by commercial growers.

Why is black polythene used instead of transparent polythene for the channels? ...Q.23

Investigation 3.1
To investigate the effect of pot size on maturity

1. When potting up tomatoes from 75 mm into 125 mm pots, leave three plants in 75 mm pots.
2. When planting out the tomato plants for the project, leave three in 125 mm pots and pot up three more in 225 mm pots.
3. Grow on the nine plants in the greenhouse, supporting them with canes inserted in the pots and removing side shoots.
4. After the first fruit has set, feed with liquid fertiliser very two weeks.
5. Record the date when each plant produces its first ripe fruit.

In the project and investigation above feeding has been recommended only after the fruit has set; the reason for this is that if feeding is begun too early tomato plants make rampant vegetative growth at the expense of fruit formation.

Many gardening experts recommend the stopping of tomato plants after a certain number of trusses have set. Whether or not this is good advice is something that could be investigated in the classroom. The author does not recommend stopping tomato plants in school greenhouses as the growing points provide material for use in the classroom during the autumn term.

Growing house plants from seed

In addition to the house plants propagated from their leaves in Book 1, many are easily grown from seed.

House plant seeds are sown in pots or boxes in the manner already described for bedding plants. Instead of pricking out from the seed tray to the plant box, houseplants are pricked out into individual pots. Some plants will mature in the original pot, others will require potting on to larger pots by the method described for tomatoes.

The most suitable houseplants to grow from seed in the school greenhouse are:

Tradescantia

Begonia

Exacum affine

Celosia

Jacaranda

Eucalyptus gunii

Thunbergia

Coleus

Impatiens

Begonia
This is a perennial with a very long flowering period. Each plant carries separate male and female flowers; when the plants become older they can be propagated by division.

Exacum affine
This annual has pretty blue flowers and very attractive foliage. As the plants are small they can be pricked out into J.I. No. 2 compost, five plants in each 125 mm pot.

Celosia
This is easily grown from seed. Seedlings are pricked out individually into 125 mm pots of J.I. No. 2 compost.

Jacaranda
A tropical tree which makes an attractive foliage plant during the first two years of its growth.

Eucalyptus gunnii
An interesting tree from Australia. When it becomes too large for use as a pot plant it should be hardened off, planted outside and cut down to one and a half metres.

Branches will grow from the top of the trunk during the summer; if this growth is cut off each autumn the tree will survive for many years. A tree grown in this manner is known as a *pollard*.

Which common indigenous tree is often grown as a pollard? ...Q.24

Thunbergia (Black-eyed Susie)
A climbing plant which flowers very freely. Seeds must be sown thinly as the cotyledons are large.

Before pricking out a wire or cane frame should be fixed over the pot to support the plant.

Coleus
An attractive foliage plant which can be grown in any size pot from 125 to 175 mm (one plant per pot). The young plant must be stopped – have its tip removed – when it is 100 mm high. Flower buds must be removed as they appear or the internodes will lengthen and the plant lose it compact habit. Coleus cuttings root readily in a beaker of water and can be used to demonstrate the genetic similarity between daughter plants and their parents.

Impatiens and Browallia
Two easy to grow, free-flowering house plants.

Mist propagation

Cuttings of many greenhouse plants are difficult to strike; in order to root these, growers have mist propagation units in their greenhouses.

A mist propagator

54 GCSE Rural Science 2

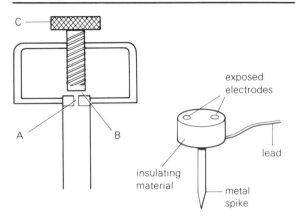

A mist propagator (right) and in section (left)

Water is forced through a very small hole A and strikes a metal plate B with considerable force. The impact shatters the water into tiny drops, which fall slowly as a mist. The size of the droplets can be adjusted by turning knob C.

The mist continues until there is enough water on the two bare electrodes of the electronic leaf to complete a circuit; when this circuit is completed a solenoid valve turns the mist off. When the electrodes dry the current stops and mist is automatically turned on again.

The rooting medium under the mist is warmed by an electric soil warming cable.

Cuttings root more quickly in a mist propagation unit because:

* The humid atmosphere keeps the leaves turgid.
* Transpiration is small, thus the cutting has no water stress.
* The water flow is cut off before any of the air spaces in the rooting medium become waterlogged.
* The temperature of the rooting medium and the atmosphere are kept at the level most suited to the plants (25°C for most plants).
* Fungus diseases associated with humid atmospheres do not appear as the spores are continually washed away.

A mist propagation unit

Protected cultivation

Project 3.4
To propagate a number of good plants from an overgrown rubber plant *(Ficus decora)*

If an overgrown rubber plant is not available in school, an appeal to parents will often provide a fair number.

Rubber plants are grown for their foliage. They are popular due to their tolerance of poor light conditions and also because they withstand long periods of drought and do not die if watering is sometimes forgotten.

1. 250 mm from the top of the plant cut a ring of bark 10 mm wide, completely encircling the stem, and remove it.
2. Make a vertical slit in the stem at the place where the bark is removed.
3. Insert a matchstick in the slit to keep it open.
4. Take a handful of peat and thoroughly wet it.
5. Plaster the wet peat around the split.
6. Cover the peat with a sheet of transparent polythene and tie top and bottom.
7. Leave for a few weeks.
8. When roots can be seen through the polythene, take a pair of secateurs and cut the stem just below the peat.
9. Remove the polythene and plant in a pot of John Innes No. 2 compost.

The new plant will be short and leafy, ideal for decorative purposes. Retain the old plant; having lost its top this plant will grow a number of lateral shoots from the nodes. When the lateral shoots are long enough treat them in a similar way to the top and obtain more good plants.

This method of propagation is known as *air layering*:

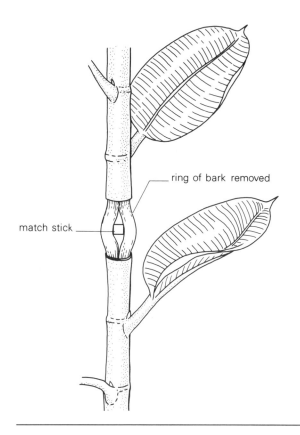
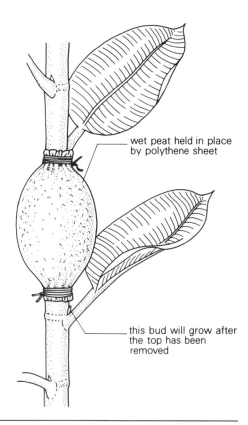

Cucumber (*Cucumis sativus*)

This plant has been cultivated in India for thousands of years. It was also grown by the Greeks and Romans. Although it is usually eaten raw in salads it can be boiled or fried and served as a vegetable. It has a high sugar and vitamin content. Cucumber is a hairy plant which climbs by means of long tendrils. Unlike the gourds, cucumbers do not have to be pollinated to make them form fruits. With indoor cucumbers it is necessary to prevent pollination, as fruits from pollinated flowers have a bitter taste. This is done in one of two ways:

1. Remove all male flowers as they appear.
2. Grow a variety which produces only female flowers.

Project 3.5
To compare different methods of growing cucumbers

Purchase some indoor cucumber seeds (not the ridge type, which are grown outside). Place the seeds on a wet paper towel in a warm room. They will quickly germinate and as soon as they do pot them up individually in 7 cm pots, using a good compost. Grow on in a heated greenhouse until the plants are ready for potting on. Fix a metal frame, or horizontal wires, as high as the roof allows, for the plants to climb. Plants should be two metres apart. Allow the shoots to climb and remove any that do not. Grow the plants in the following ways:

1. In a grow-bag (one plant per bag).
2. In a previously soaked and fertilised bale of straw.
3. In a soil bed.
4. In 10 litres of compost piled on a concrete floor. As the plant grows add more compost to the pile.
5. By a method which you have thought of yourself.

Cucumbers growing in a school greenhouse

Pepper

The word 'pepper' refers to two quite different groups of plants. The hot pepper, which is often used with salt as a 'condiment', consists of ground peppercorns from a tropical climbing plant. The large fleshy fruits we call sweet peppers grow on a bushy plant of the genus *Capsicum*. In this section the pepper we refer to is the latter one.

Sweet pepper (*Capsicum annuum*)

As the scientific name suggests this is an annual plant. A native of America, the plant is half hardy and is usually grown in unheated greenhouses. It is a small bush which fruits continuously for up to three months. As they ripen the fruits turn red or yellow according to variety. Green peppers are unripe fruit. The vitamin C content is very high.

Peppers produce fruit throughout the summer – a good yield can be obtained before the summer holidays by the following method:

1. At the end of February sow seeds individually in peat blocks or Jiffy 7s.
2. Keep in the classroom until emergence.

3. Transfer the block, complete with seedling, to a 7 cm pot filled with a good quality compost.
4. Grow on in a heated greenhouse, or on the classroom window sill with foil to reflect the light (see p. 47). (A 'grow-lamp', which uses a mercury vapour lamp, hung directly over the plants will help to prevent them from getting drawn. However, in the author's experience good plants cannot be grown using only 'grow-lamps'; some natural daylight is necessary.)
5. When the pots are full of roots, transfer to an unheated greenhouse and plant up in full sized grow-bags – two plants per bag.
6. Once the bushes are established and growing vigorously, feed each week with a tomato fertiliser.
7. Remove the fruits with a sharp knife when they are large enough to use.

Aphids can be a problem with peppers. The author has never used any pesticide for over 20 years and finds that well-grown plants can carry an aphid population with no ill effect, indeed a small population of aphids is necessary to maintain predator populations. If you decide to use a systemic pesticide to control aphids on peppers remember that the same sap which kills the aphid is present in the fruit which is to be eaten. The presence of aphids on the plant does not mean that the pesticide has gone – you may have bred a resistant strain.

Micropropagation

Micropropagation is also known as 'tissue culture' and is the propagation of new plants from a minute part of a parent plant.

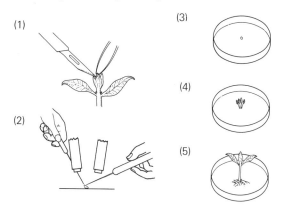

(1) Using sterile forceps and scalpel a tiny part of the growing tip of the plant to be propagated is removed.

(2) With the aid of a microscope the scales which surround the growing tip are removed.
(3) Just the tip is placed on an agar plate which contains nutrients and growth hormones. The actual mix of nutrients and hormones varies according to species.
(4) The tip produces many shoots.

(5) The shoots are transferred to individual agar plates which contain root hormones. The shoots then produce roots. The tiny plant can be potted up and will develop into a normal plant genetically identical to the parent.

Micropropagation is being used to grow a large range of pot plants and one firm is producing 70 000 plants each week by this method.

A very big advantage of micropropagation is that the plants produced in this way are virus free. Marrows and beans are being grown free from virus mosiac diseases by this method.

Virus free potatoes can also be grown by micropropagation. This crop is a little different, however, as roots are produced without the addition of hormone. The production of virus free tubers to be used as seed is extremely difficult and it takes four years to produce 7000 plants from an individual virus free potato by traditional methods. Micropropagation can produce 7000 plants in only five months from a single virus free potato. It is also possible to grow tubers which are only 5 mm in diameter by micro techniques. Tubers this size may one day be used as 'seed' potatoes instead of the full-sized ones which we now use.

Pests and diseases in the greenhouse

Many of the pests and diseases which affect crop plants outside also affect greenhouse plants; in addition there are a number of pests and diseases which are specific to greenhouses.

Greenhouse whitefly (*Trialeurodes vaporariorum*)

A common pest of greenhouse plants is a small white fly only 1 mm long. The body is yellow, the eyes black, and the wings white. The adult flies spend most of their time on the underside of leaves but will take off if disturbed.

Both adults and larvae feed by sucking sap from the leaves of plants; the loss of sap weakens the plants and reduces their growth. In addition the insects excrete a sticky substance (honeydew), rich in sugar, which interferes with the normal function of the leaf. A black fungus grows in the honeydew, spoiling the appearance of the plants and fruit and preventing light from reaching the leaves.

Tomatoes, cucumbers, chrysanthemum, dahlia, fuschia, salvia and many more are subject to whitefly attack.

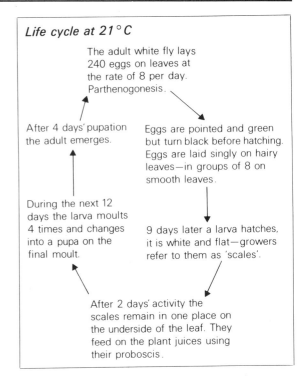

Life cycle at 21°C

The adult white fly lays 240 eggs on leaves at the rate of 8 per day. Parthenogenesis.

Eggs are pointed and green but turn black before hatching. Eggs are laid singly on hairy leaves—in groups of 8 on smooth leaves.

9 days later a larva hatches, it is white and flat—growers refer to them as 'scales'.

After 2 days' activity the scales remain in one place on the underside of the leaf. They feed on the plant juices using their proboscis.

During the next 12 days the larva moults 4 times and changes into a pupa on the final moult.

After 4 days' pupation the adult emerges.

Control

1. *Prevention*: any plant taken into a pest-free greenhouse should be carefully checked for

Whitefly on tomato leaves

whitefly. Weeds, upon which whitefly can overwinter, shold be removed from the greenhouse. As whitefly can survive mild winters outside the greenhouse, all weeds around it should be strictly controlled.

2. *Biological control* (using one organism to control another): many years ago a Hampshire gardener discovered whitefly larvae which were black on the leaves of his tomato plants. He sent the leaves with the black larvae to a horticultural research station where they found that, instead of producing whitefly, a black larva produced a tiny wasp. Observing the female wasp they found that she visited about 50 whitefly larvae during her 14 day life, and laid an egg in each one. Inside each larva the egg hatched into a wasp larva which consumed the insides of the whitefly larva, killing it and turning it black. The wasp larva pupated inside the whitefly, and emerged as an adult a few days later.

The wasp was named *Encarsia formosa* and during the 1930s it was widely used to assist whitefly control in greenhouses. During the 1940s new insecticides were discovered and the use of *Encarsia formosa* was discontinued. More recently the dangers of the liberal use of insecticides have been realised and once more *Encarsia formosa* is being used to control whitefly in greenhouses.

It is possible to buy tobacco plant leaves upon which are whitefly larvae which contain the parasite *Encarsia formosa*. These are hung in the greenhouse above the whitefly infested plants; a few days later the wasps emerge and begin laying eggs in the whitefly scales.

What would be the result if *Encarsia formosa* **destroyed all the whitefly in a greenhouse?**
...Q.25

3. *Chemical control*: Insecticides can be applied to the plants in the form of dusts or sprays but the most effective method of applying insecticides in a controlled environment like a greenhouse is by smoke fumigation. A smoke capsule (similar to a firework), when lit, produces a large volume of smoke which carries the insecticide. Each capsule will discharge a certain volume of smoke, so it is necessary to know the volume of the greenhouse before fumigation in order to use the correct number of capsules. Most insecticides kill only the adult forms of whitefly and treatment has to be repeated three or four times at seven day intervals if good control is to be achieved.

How many 440 m^3 capsules will be required to fumigate a greenhouse 8 m wide, 2 m to eaves, 3.5 m to ridge and 80 m long?
...Q.26

Red spider mite (*Tetranychus urticae*, and *T. cinnabarinus*)

Red spider mite is a serious pest in many greenhouses where the environmental conditions required for the crop are similar to the conditions favourable to red spider.

The red spider is an arachnid (the class of invertebrates that includes spiders, mites and scorpions) with two parts to its body and eight legs. They are just visible without magnification, their oval bodies being about 0.6 mm in length. The adults are green, yellow or red and are most easily seen as they cross from one leaf to another on the mass of web which they spin.

Damage
The red spider mite damages a wide range of plants including chrysanthemums, impatiens, asparagus, and salvia. The damage is caused in two ways: (a) the spider mite spins thick webs which cover the leaves and stems of the plants, cutting off light and preventing air movement; (b) the spider mites feed on the underside of leaves in large numbers. The upper surfaces of the infected leaves develop a fine yellow speckling; later the leaves turn yellow and hard. Badly infested plants lose their vigour, become yellow and die.

Life cycle
Eggs are laid on the lower surface of the leaves and protected with the fine webbing. Nymphs feed on the leaves and moult twice before becoming adult. The time from egg to adult varies greatly with temperature; at 35°C it is six days whilst at 10°C it is sixty days. *T. cinnabarinus*

breeds throughout the year. *T. urticae* stops breeding when daylight is less than 14 hours; the males die and the females turn brick red, leave the plants and find a tiny crevice in which to hibernate. The hibernation ends in March and the females return to the plant.

Control
1. *Hygiene*: Red spider sometimes survives on weeds outside the greenhouse, but proper control of weeds around the greenhouse should eliminate this. New stocks of plants should be given a period of isolation, to ensure they are free from red spider, before being placed in an uninfected greenhouse. Old crops should be removed as soon as possible and destroyed. If an infected crop is due for completion in October the lights in the greenhouse should be lit for two hours at dusk, each night from the end of August.

How will lighting the greenhouse help control red spider mite? ...Q.27

2. *Environmental conditions*: Red spider mites will only thrive in hot, dry conditions; their numbers can be considerably reduced by spraying plants with clean water once or twice each day.
3. *Biological control*: A predatory mite *Phytoseiulus persimilis* gives excellent control of red spider if it is introduced early in the year. The mite cannot survive without its prey and is usually lost during the winter; new stocks must therefore be purchased each spring from a breeder.

How does this mite control red spider? ...Q.28

The predatory mite *Phytoseiulus persimilis* is susceptible to most pesticides and will be killed if these are used to control other pests, such as aphids, leaving red spider mite to multiply unchecked.

Why does the same pesticide fail to kill the red spider mite? ...Q.29

4. *Chemical control*: chemicals which control arachnids are called *acaricides* and can be applied as dusts, sprays or smokes. Some of the available chemicals, like dicofol, destroy all stages of the mite including the eggs and adults, whilst others kill only adults leaving the immature stages unharmed.

In theory a single application of dicofol or two applications of a chemical which kills only one stage, made at suitable intervals, will clear a greenhouse of red spider. In practice there are many strains of red spider that are immune to the effects of some toxic chemicals and several different acaricides have to be used either separately or together, depending upon the manufacturer's instructions.

The environment in most school greenhouses does not suit red spider mite; if you are 'lucky' enough to have a few infected plants they should be retained for study.

Fungus diseases in greenhouses

There are several fungus diseases which appear in greenhouses; the most common is damping-off of seedlings. This is caused by the fungus *Pythium* which grows in the hypocotyls of seedlings causing them to collapse; the spore producing bodies of *Pythium* can be seen at the base of patches of collapsed seedlings as a grey mould. Correct watering is the best method of control; too much water on seedlings (particularly lettuce) creates ideal conditions for damping-off.

Other methods of control are watering with a fungicide – Cheshunt compound or thiram – or killing the *Pythium* spores by soil sterilisation.

Questions: Protected cultivation

1. Write single sentences to answer the following questions:
   (a) What is a greenhouse?
   (b) Why is it necessary to harden off plants?
   (c) Why are seedlings handled only by the cotyledon?
   (d) Why is John Innes No. 1 compost unsuitable for potting up tomatoes?
   (e) How is the temperature of the rooting medium maintained in a mist propagation unit?
   (f) Which parasitic wasp is used in the 'biological control' of whitefly?

(g) What material is prepared by stacking turf upside-down?
(h) Why is it that some tomato flowers fail to develop into fruit?
(i) What is the advantage of using hoof and horn rather than sulphate of ammonia to supply nitrogen to J.I. compost?
(j) Name two environmental conditions which are controlled in a greenhouse.

2. (a) Give two reasons why it is often warmer inside an unheated greenhouse than it is outside.
   (b) (i) Describe with words and diagrams how the soil in a greenhouse bed may be heated.
       (ii) What are the advantages of warming a greenhouse bed?
   (c) Explain the purpose of the earth wire in greenhouse electrical appliances.

3. You have a greenhouse which you wish to heat.
   (a) Name three fuels which could be used.
   (b) Describe in detail four steps which you would take to minimise heating costs.

4. Two identical greenhouses were each planted up with 200 Eurocross tomato plants. In greenhouse A the tomatoes were grown by nutrient film technique. In greenhouse B grow-bags were used (two plants per bag). The grow-bags cost £1.50 each. The running costs for greenhouse A were £840 and for greenhouse B were £650. 1900 kg of fruit was harvested from greenhouse A and 1600 kg from greenhouse B, the average price obtained was 70 p per kilo of tomatoes.
   (a) How much profit (or loss) was made in each greenhouse?
   (b) What is nutrient film technique?
   (c) What is a grow-bag?
   (d) Suggest possible reasons why the crop was greater with nutrient film than with grow-bags.
   (e) Why were the running costs greater for nutrient film than for grow-bags?
   (f) Which conditions would be most difficult to control in the attempt to keep conditions for the two groups of plants identical?

5. Cuttings were taken from: geraniums, *Coleus*, *Tradescantia*, *Plumbago*, *Sanseveria*, Ivy and *Impatiens*. Half of the cuttings were treated with rooting hormone and half were not.

Results:

	Percentage which rooted	
	Treated	Untreated
Geranium	50	50
Coleus	98	74
Tradescantia	95	86
Plumbago	43	21
Sansevertia	32	27
Ivy	94	90
Impatiens	95	96

   (a) Display the results on two bar graphs.
   (b) What conclusions can be drawn from this experiment?
   (c) Design a further experiment to test the effectiveness of the rooting powder.

6. (a) Describe a polythene tunnel as used by growers.
   (b) List the advantages and the disadvantages a polythene tunnel has when compared with a greenhouse.
   n.b. A greenhouse costs five times as much as a similar size polythene tunnel.

7. (a) What do you understand by humidity?
   (b) In what ways can very high humidity in a greenhouse be harmful to plants?
   (c) Explain the effect that changing humidity has upon the transpiration rate of plants in the greenhouse.
   (d) Describe methods of increasing and reducing humidity in a greenhouse.
   (e) Why is it that the very high humidity maintained in a mist propagation system does not encourage fungal growth?

4 Fruit

Indigenous fruit is divided into two main culture groups: top fruits and soft fruits.

Top fruits grow on trees, and soft fruits grow on canes, bushes or herbaceous plants.

Task 4.1

Draw two columns; head one column 'Top fruit' and the other column 'Soft fruit'. Enter the following list of fruits in the correct columns: apple, strawberry, loganberry, cherry, damson, gooseberry, pear, black currant, raspberry, blackberry, plum, red currant, peach. Turn to the end of the chapter and check your answer.

Soft fruit

Strawberry *(Fragaria chiloensis)*

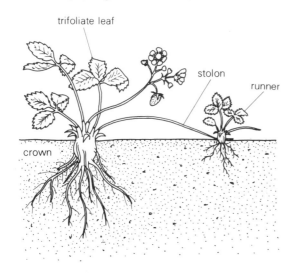

The cultivated strawberry was not bred from our native wild strawberry *(Fragaria vesca)* but is a hybrid of two American species *F. virginiana* and *F. chiloensis*.

Unlike other British soft fruit the strawberry plant has no woody stems, but is a low-growing, hardy, herbaceous perennial. The fruit consists of a swollen receptacle with seeds attached to the outside.

Where are the seeds in other fruits? ...Q.1

Strawberry flowers are self-fertile and will pollinate without the insects which are often seen visiting the plants.

Growing strawberries
It is better to begin growing strawberries from purchased, certified plants than to accept gifts of plants propagated by well-meaning friends. Certified stock will produce fruit for three or four years, but plants raised by amateurs will probably be infected with virus and other diseases. In Scotland it is illegal to sell strawberry plants that have not been certified healthy by the Ministry of Agriculture.

As with other fruit there are many different clones (varieties). Cambridge Favourite is an excellent variety but local advice should be sought when deciding which to grow, as it is important to have plants which suit local conditions.

Site
Choose a sheltered part of the site, taking care to avoid any frost pockets or hollows which are known to exist. Frost damages open flowers, but a complete loss of crop from frost is unlikely, as

the plant flowers over a four week period. Also, buds and fruit are more frost resistant than open flowers.

Soil
Any well drained soil will grow strawberries; good preparation is essential as the crop is to remain in the ground for three or four years. Deep cultivation by double digging or bastard trenching (see Book 2) with a heavy dressing of farmyard manure (6 kg/m^2) will improve drainage and provide all the nitrogen, phosphate and potash requirement for the first year. The soil must be completely free from perennial weeds.

Name a perennial grass that may be troublesome.
...Q.2

Strawberries will tolerate fairly acid conditions and lime should not be added as excess of calcium can cause deficiencies of magnesium and iron.

Planting
Providing the ground is frost free, planting can be done at any time of year from July to the following May. The best time to plant is from July to September.

Why is this the best time to plant? ...Q.3

Plants should be spaced 400 mm apart with 750 mm between the rows. A hole large enough to allow the roots to spread is dug with a trowel; the roots are arranged before returning the soil and pressing down firmly. Care must be taken not to bury the crown, which should be at soil level:

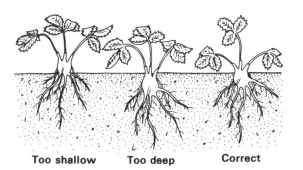
Too shallow   Too deep   Correct

Culture
Control weeds throughout the season by shallow hoeing with a dutch hoe.

As the fruits develop put a good layer of straw underneath and all around the plant. The straw keeps the berries off the soil and prevents them from becoming rain-splashed. If no straw is available black polythene can be used. Strawing too early in the season disrupts the night flow of warm air from the soil and the possibility of frost is increased.

After the first year potash may be in short supply; a dressing of muriate of potash at the rate of 5 g/m^2 during the autumn will correct this.

Break off runners as they appear.

Harvesting
Harvest by picking the berries as soon as they ripen, taking also the calyx and a length of stalk. Unless the crop is carefully covered with a net, birds – blackbirds, thrushes and linnets in particular – will eat the berries as they ripen.

After harvest
When the last fruit has been gathered, clip off all leaves and runners with sharp shears, taking care not to damage the crowns. Rake off the debris, including the straw, and burn it. Lightly fork between the rows to break the trodden soil surface.

Crop duration
A well-maintained strawberry bed will give a worthwhile crop for three or four years; the older plants produce more but smaller fruit. At the end of its useful life the plants are dug from the strawberry bed as soon as the last fruit is gathered; this allows another crop of a different kind to be grown the same season. The new strawberry bed is planted on a different site.

Why not plant the new bed on the same site as the old one? ...Q.4

Propagation
Strawberries propagate themselves by growing stolons with very long internodes. Each node grows into a new plant.

A strawberry runner

Task 4.2

1. Before the end of the summer term fill a 75 mm pot with John Innes No. 2 potting compost.
2. Select a good stolon growing from a strawberry plant and sink the pot in the soil beneath the first node of the stolon.
3. Use a piece of wire shaped like a large hairpin to hold the node over the centre of the pot.
4. Cut the stolon beyond the first node to prevent it growing further.
5. By September the runner will have formed a new plant rooting in the pot. Cut the stolon connecting the runner to the old plant and lift the pot.
6. *Either* remove the plant from pot and compost, examine and draw.
   Or pot on into a 125 mm pot and grow in a cool greenhouse or window-sill, to produce flowers and fruit for examination the following spring.

Pests and diseases of strawberries

In addition to birds (and slugs) eating the ripe fruit, there are insect, mite and eelworm pests as well as fungus and virus diseases which cause crop reduction or crop failure.

Aphids: The strawberry aphid (*Chaetosiphon fragafolii*) causes little or no feeding damage but is important as a vector for virus diseases.

What is a vector? ...Q.5

The shallot aphid *(Myzus ascalonicus)* winters in the crowns of strawberry plants and can cause considerable damage, particularly during a mild winter. The aphid migrates to other plants in May leaving the strawberries with distorted leaves and stunted growth.

Growers control aphids with various systemic insecticides. Most amateur gardeners use malathion dust.

Nematodes (eelworms): A number of different species of nematodes infest the stems and leaves of strawberries causing distortion. Control is by the use of healthy stocks, as infected stocks are extremely difficult to clear of nematodes.

A free living soil nematode feeds on the roots of strawberries; this species does no apparent damage but is important as a vector of virus diseases.

A fungus disease – Red core (Phytophthora infestans): This disease first appeared in Scotland in 1921 and has since spread throughout the United Kingdom. The fungus attacks the roots of plants causing them to rot. The fibrous roots are destroyed; if the main roots are cut lengthways the stele appears red, hence the name. The plant above the infected roots is dwarfed and usually dies.

Red core is spread by runners from infected plants before they show any obvious signs of disease. Resting an infected field from strawberries is of little use as the fungus forms spores which remain viable in the soil for over fifteen years.

Red core can be controlled by good husbandry:
1. Always use certified stocks.
2. Only grow strawberries in well-drained soils.
3. Use varieties of strawberries which are most resistant, e.g. Cambridge Vigour, or Talisman.

Raspberry *(Rubus idaeus)*

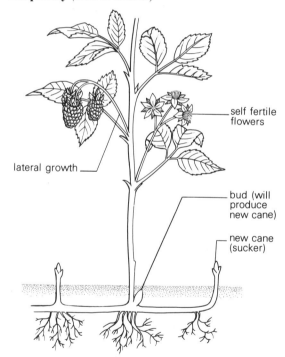

The fruit of the raspberry consists of many single-seeded drupelets closely packed around a conical receptacle. When gathered, the fruit cluster comes away leaving the receptacle attached to the plant.

The raspberry produces biennial woody canes from stools:

The underground parts of the raspberry (rootstock) remain alive producing new canes as 'suckers' each year. A row of raspberry canes will last for 20 or more years. In practice few rows survive for more than half this time due to a number of virus diseases.

Growing raspberries

Raspberries are almost always grown in rows supported by two horizontal wires, stretched between two posts 1.5 m tall:

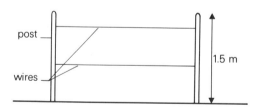

Site

Flowering somewhat later than strawberries, raspberries are less likely to suffer from spring frosts. Shelter from strong winds increases yield as cold spring winds reduce lateral growth. If planted on a slope the rows should run down rather than across the slope to allow better movement of cold night air.

Soil

Any deep well drained soil with a pH between 5 and 7 will support raspberries. Waterlogged soils and soils with a pH over 7 (calcareous soils) must be avoided.

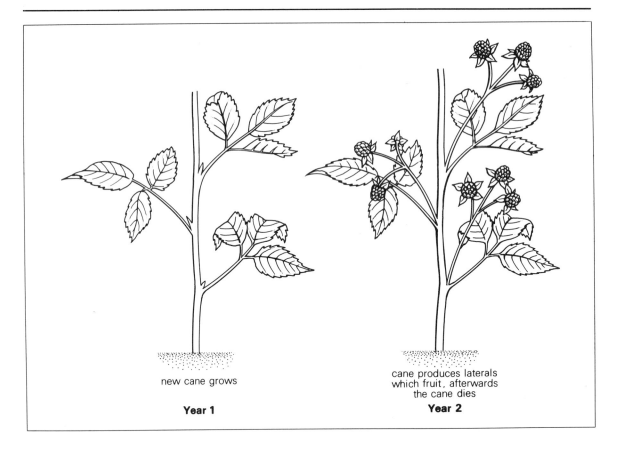

new cane grows
Year 1

cane produces laterals which fruit, afterwards the cane dies
Year 2

The soil must be free from all perennial weeds and a heavy dressing of farmyard manure should be worked in the top two spits a few months before planting.

Planting
Canes can be planted at any frost free time during the winter. Certified canes are purchased and planted to a depth of 75 mm, 450 mm apart. After the soil is firmed, the canes are cut down to leave them 250 mm high. Cutting off the canes prevents fruiting during the first season; this ensures that the total energy of the plant is used to establish a good rootstock and grow quality canes.

Culture (of an established row)
Apply 20 g/m² of sulphate of potash each spring, followed by a layer of compost or well-rotted strawy manure spread over the surface of the soil to a depth of 100 mm on either side of the row. A layer of organic material placed on the soil surface is called a *mulch*.

A mulch has the following effects:

1. It keeps the soil moist in summer.
2. It provides a supply of humus-forming material for the soil.

Which soil animal will pull the pieces of straw, etc., into the soil? ...Q.6

3. It keeps roots cool in summer and warm in winter.
4. It prevents the growth of many annual weeds.
5. It provides a supply of nutrients.

Harvesting
Fruits are picked as they ripen by gently pulling them from the receptacle; the fruit must be in dry condition as wet fruit quickly becomes mouldy. To prevent losses by birds, raspberries are often grown in a cage made from posts and plastic netting.

Pruning

After fruiting a row of raspberries is pruned as follows:

1. Using secateurs the old canes are cut off just above ground level and the strings attaching them to the horizontal wires are cut. Old canes are removed and burned.
2. Weak new canes and those growing more than 200 mm from the row are also removed.
3. The best new canes are selected and tied 100 mm apart to the two horizontal wires.
4. The unused canes are cut off at ground level and removed.

Task 4.3

1. Nail two strips of wood to the end of a wooden seed tray to represent the posts at the end of a row of raspberries.
2. Fill the tray with coarse sand.
3. Tie two horizontal strings between the 'posts', one at the top and one half way down.
4. Using apple prunings to represent raspberry canes, put a row of canes between the posts and secure to the strings with short lengths of copper wire.
5. Scrape the bark from a bunch of apple prunings and press them into the sand near to the row, to represent new raspberry canes.
6. The model now represents a row of raspberry canes before they are pruned.
7. Use a pair of secateurs to prune the 'raspberries' as described in the text above.

Pests and diseases of raspberries

The raspberry beetle (Byturus tomentosus)
The larva of the raspberry beetle feeds on the maturing fruit, causing it to become shrivelled and malformed. In addition, the presence of white larvae in gathered fruit makes it unsaleable.

Life cycle: Adult beetles hibernate in the soil and emerge during May. They fly to the flowers, feed upon them and lay their eggs, and from each egg a larva hatches. The larvae feed on the surface of the fruit and as it ripens tunnel into the receptacle. They leave one fruit and feed on another, damaging the drupelets near to the calyx. Fully grown larvae (8 mm long) pupate in the soil, producing an adult that emerges the following year.

Control: Sprays or dusts of malathion or derris when the first fruits are turning pink give effective control. Malathion is toxic to bees and must on no account be used if there are open blossoms.

Sprays and soft fruit

99.5 per cent of all commercially grown soft fruit is sprayed at least once with an agricultural chemical. When man grows crops he upsets the balance of nature; growers who grow large areas of a single crop (i.e. practise monoculture with no crop rotation) soon become dependent upon sprays. In a school garden with a wide range of plants, spraying is unnecessary and if a strict policy of no pesticides is maintained almost anything can be grown. There will be lots of insects in the garden but natural predation will prevent large populations of individual species from building up to pest proportions. Remember that all animal life (including ourselves) depends upon the green plant. If we are to have a rich wildlife in this country we must not become alarmed if birds share our fruit, caterpillars have a little of our cabbage and aphids suck some sap from our roses.

Blackcurrants
(Ribes nigrum)

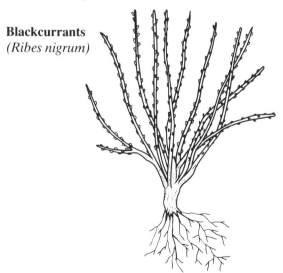

Although the flowers are self-fertile, pollinating insects, particularly bumble bees, are important and have a marked influence upon yield.

Growing blackcurrants
Some blackcurrant bushes appear more or less normal but fail to crop due to a virus condition called *reversion*. For this reason only bushes certified healthy by the Ministry of Agriculture should be planted.

Site
Blackcurrants are gross feeders and require a deep soil well supplied with nutrients and having good reserves of water. They require freedom from late spring frosts and shelter from strong, cold winds.

Soil
The soil must be completely free from perennial weeds. Blackcurrants do not thrive on very alkaline or very acid soils – 6.5 being the ideal pH value.

What substance is added to the soil to increase the pH? ...Q.7

Ten kilograms of well-rooted farmyard manure should be dug into each square metre of soil, working it to a depth of two spits several months before planting.

Planting
Bushes may be planted at any time from October to March providing the soil is frost free; earlier plantings are better as the warm soil encourages root development.

Bushes raised in individual containers (flimsy plastic pots) may be planted at other times of the year.

Why is it possible to plant a container-grown plant in June when transplanting from a bed is not recommended? ...Q.8

Blackcurrant bushes are planted two metres apart. They should be 150 mm deeper in the soil than they were when lifted (see diagram, page 69).

1. A hole large enough to accommodate the roots is dug.
2. The plant is held in position and the roots carefully arranged.
3. Fine soil is put over and around the roots and the hole filled.
4. The soil is trodden firmly around the plant.
5. Each branch is cut off leaving only one bud above the soil.
6. The surface is levelled with a rake.

Culture
The new bush will not fruit during its first year, its energy being used to devlop a good root system and grow strong branches, to bear next year's fruit.

The soil is kept weed-free with the dutch hoe. After the first year an annual dressing of complete fertiliser (10:10:18) is applied in early spring at the rate of 10 g/m^2.

Which nutrient would be lost if this fertiliser was applied in the autumn? ...Q.9

In addition, a mulch of well-rotted manure or compost is applied in the autumn.

Harvest
The fruit is gathered as it ripens, either by removing individual berries or by picking whole strigs.

Blackcurrants must not be harvested when they are wet.

Pruning
This operation may be carried out soon after harvesting the fruit or it may be done during the dormant season.

The bark of new growth is light in colour; one year old bark is a little darker; two years old bark is darker, and so on, until 5 years old – by which time the bark is black.

Old wood can be cut out without removing all the new, as a properly maintained bush will have vigorous new growths arising from the base of the plant, or from buds under the soil.

Propagation
Propagation is by *hardwood cuttings*:

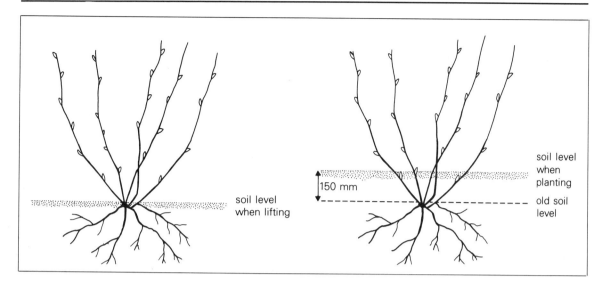

1. In autumn select a strong shoot of the current year's growth.
2. Remove the top, weaker, growth making a correct pruning cut with a pair of secateurs (see below right).
3. Make the cutting about 200 mm long by removing the bottom with a straight cut, just below a bud.
4. Use a spade to make a cleft in the soil 200 mm deep.
5. Half fill the cleft with coarse sand.
6. Insert the cuttings 150 mm apart, taking great care not to damage any buds. Leave two buds above the surface.
7. Fill in the cleft.
8. By the following autumn the cuttings will be rooted and may be planted in their permanent positions.

Old, neglected blackcurrant bushes can sometimes be rejuvenated by cutting them off just above the ground.

What other action would you take to rejuvenate the bush? ...Q.10

Task 4.4

1. Take four tie-on labels and label as shown:

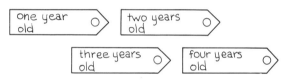

2. Examine an established dormant blackcurrant bush and tie each label on to the correct age of wood.
3. Take a number of short lengths of string.
4. Tie one length of string on to each part of the bush in the exact postion where you think a pruning cut ought to be made.

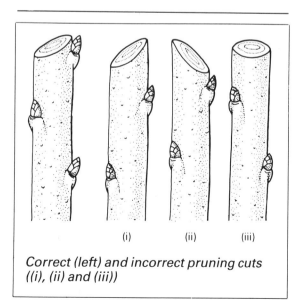

Correct (left) and incorrect pruning cuts ((i), (ii) and (iii))

Pests and diseases of blackcurrants
Aphids, red spiders, midges, and other pests affect blackcurrant bushes but the most serious pest is a gall mite.

Blackcurrant gall mite (Eriophyes ribes): The gall mites can be seen inside infected buds with the aid of a hand lens. They enter the buds of the blackcurrant in June and July and feed inside.

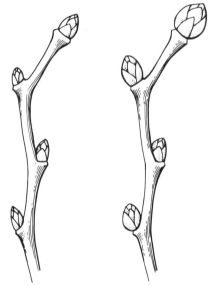

Healthy blackcurrant buds (left), and buds infested with gall mite (right)

The buds gradually lose their pointed shape and swell up, giving the mite its common name 'big bud mite'. In early spring the mites leave the old buds and search for new ones. Some mites are carried by insects or wind to other bushes, spreading the infection. Spraying with 1% lime sulphur, just before the flowers open, and repeating four weeks later gives some measure of control. Hand picking and burning the big buds may also help reduce the infestation. Badly infected bushes should be dug up and burned.

The gall mite causes loss of buds but the main damage the mite does is as a vector of the virus disease reversion.

Reversion: Reversion is a virus disease of black currant bushes, causing serious crop reduction.
There are two visible symptoms of reversion:

1. The flower buds are a red colour instead of the usual grey.
2. The leaf changes shape:

Healthy blackcurrant leaf (left) and one from a bush infected with reversion (right)

What three differences can be seen in the two leaves? ...Q.11

Control is by only planting bushes propagated from certified healthy stock and digging up and burning infected plants.

Top fruit

Apples *(Malus pumila)*

Apples are the most widely grown top fruit in the United Kingdom. In addition to millions of garden trees, 50 000 hectares are grown commercially. Large orchards are restricted to areas where the site, climate and soil is most suitable.

Site
The ideal site is between sea level and 100 metres, on a gentle concave slope giving good air drainage and avoiding spring frosts. The direction of the slope should be such as to avoid gales and salt winds.

Climate
Summer rainfall should not exceed 400 mm, because too much rain makes the control of fungus disease difficult. An average daily temperature in July and August about 20°C is best

and temperatures in winter should not be excessively cold. Good periods of sunshine during late summer are needed to ripen the fruit.

Soil

A deep soil in excellent condition allows the roots to develop and have ample water, air and nutrients. Trees soon die in waterlogged soils. The soil needs to be slightly acid (pH 6–6.5) as apples cannot extract iron or magnesium from alkaline soils. In practice, a wide range of soils from sandy loams to clay loams are suitable for apple trees. Light shallow soils do not retain sufficient moisture and heavy clays often have drainage defects.

The apple tree

Almost all apple trees are two different trees joined together; the roots are of one type and the stem and branches are another. The clone that bears the best fruit often grows into an unsuitable tree if standing upon its own roots. By giving his favourite apples the roots of his choice man can grow them on sizes and shapes of trees to suit his needs; he can also make them bear fruit much earlier than they otherwise would. The join is always above soil level otherwise the top part may produce its own unsatisfactory roots and the rootstock die away:

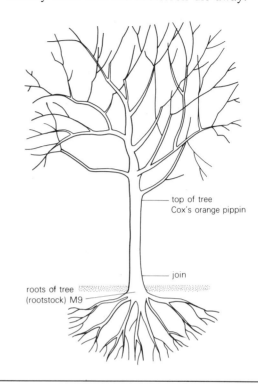

Project 4.1
To grow a single column apple tree

1. Pot up an apple rootstock (M26 or MM106) in a 24 cm container filled with good quality compost.
2. Take a bud from a single column apple tree and using the method described for roses on page 90 carry out a budding operation. This is best done in the classroom with the container on a table to give a convenient working height.
3. Take the tree back to the garden and plunge the container into the soil. Water as necessary.
4. The following spring when the new bud is growing, cut the root stock off just above the bud. Remove any rootstock buds if they begin to grow.
5. In the autumn plant the new tree into its final position.

Note: Single column apple trees do not form branches and therefore require no pruning. As they can be planted just one metre apart they are ideal subjects for small gardens. For single column apple trees contact: Institute of Horticultural Research, East Malling, Kent.

A number of the apple rootstocks available grow small trees, some grow very large trees and others grow trees of intermediate size. The East Malling Research Station, Kent and the John Innes Institute at Merton, Surrey, have jointly produced a series of rootstocks called Malling-

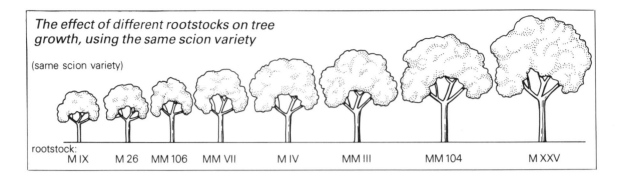

The effect of different rootstocks on tree growth, using the same scion variety

(same scion variety)

rootstock: M IX, M 26, MM 106, MM VII, M IV, MM III, MM 104, M XXV

Merton which are numbered in sequence with the prefix MM.

In addition to the size of the tree the rootstock influences the period of cropping and the resistance the tree has to disease.

What other factors influence the size of tree?
...Q.12

The variety is joined to the rootstock by budding or grafting. Budding is more widely used than grafting and is similar to the budding of roses described in Chapter 5.

Growing rootstocks
Rootstocks for apples are grown from hardwood cuttings or in a stoolbed which is another method of vegetative propagation.

Why are rootstocks not raised from seed?
...Q.13

Stooling
A rootstock (A, below) is allowed to grow for a season. During the winter it is cut to within 25 mm of the ground. (B) The following spring a number of shoots grow. (C) When about 150 mm tall these are earthed up with a draw hoe to cover half their stems. The shoots continue to grow and are earthed up twice more during the season. (D) The soil around the base encourages rooting and each shoot develops an independent root system.

In November the soil is removed and each shoot complete with roots is cut from the parent stock by secateurs. The rooted shoots are planted out singly and will be available for grafting or budding.

The old stool will produce a further crop of shoots the following year and, if properly cared for, will remain in production for a further twenty years.

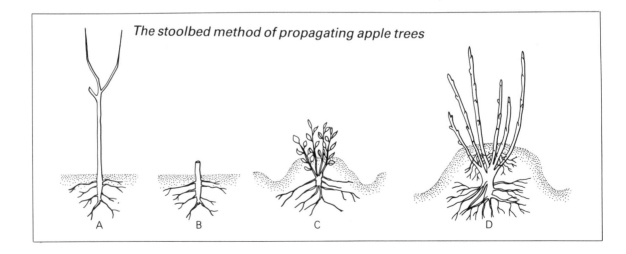

The stoolbed method of propagating apple trees

Whip and tongue graft

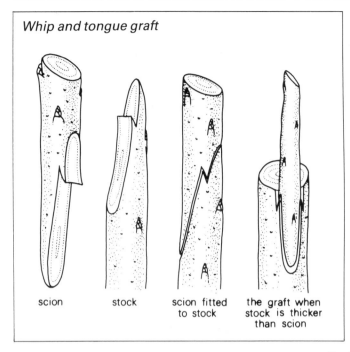

scion · stock · scion fitted to stock · the graft when stock is thicker than scion

Saddle graft

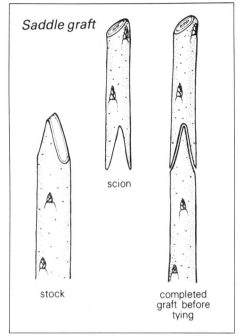

scion

stock · completed graft before tying

Grafting Strictly speaking, grafting is not a method of propagating apple trees as it merely changes the variety of a tree.

In order to graft, a piece of new growth called the *scion* is taken from a dormant tree and attached to a rootstock in such a way that the cambium layers of each are brought into contact. Grafting is done in spring before the scion breaks dormancy (this is artificially delayed by collecting scions some time before grafting).

Grafts are secured with raffia and sealed with a coat of wax, bitumen or rubber latex, specially produced for the purpose.

The above grafts can be practised in the classroom by clamping an apple pruning in a stand and grafting another apple pruning to it.

These practice grafts will not of course grow. To make a graft in the classroom that will grow perform the following task:

Task 4.5

1. Plant a potato in a 225 mm pot filled with John Innes No. 2 compost.
2. Leave the pot in a greenhouse, or a very light place in the classroom, until it has grown and has stems over 5 mm thick.
3. Cut tomato side shoots that are similar in thickness to the potato stems, and take them to the classroom.
4. Place the tomato shoot on a sterile bench and thoroughly wash your hands.
5. Use a sterile razor blade (in a suitable holder) or a sterile scalpel and, making a horizontal cut, remove all but 50 mm of a potato stem.
6. Cut the bottom of the tomato stem into a tapering wedge making only one clean cut on each side.
7. Make a vertical cut in the centre of the potato stem and fit in the tomato. As far as is possible ensure that the cambium layer of the scion is making contact with the cambium layer of the rootstock.
8. Carefully tie with raffia, avoiding any damage to the delicate tissue.
9. Graft tomato on to the other stems using different methods, for example try the saddle graft, or the whip and tongue graft (without the tongue).

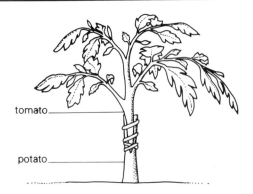

10. Cover with a ploche and leave in a light place but NOT in direct sunlight.
11. One week later open the ploche vents.
12. When the grafts have taken, remove the ploche and grow on in the greenhouse.

It is possible that the resulting plant will produce both tomatoes and potatoes; these are good to eat.

Caution: Never graft tomato on to other solanums (e.g. tobacco, henbane and deadly nightshade), or the fruit they produce may be very poisonous.

A tomato plant grafted to the roots of a potato

Tree shapes

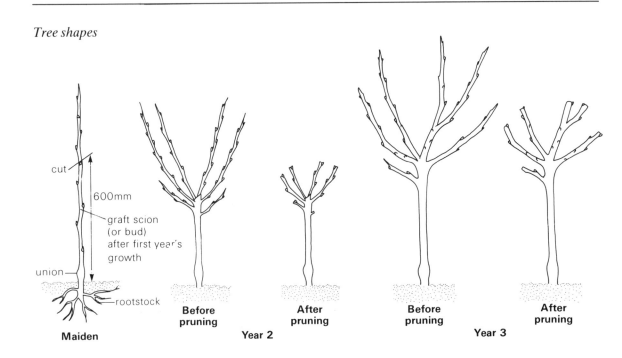

Fruit

The rootstock and environmental conditions determine the growth, vigour and ultimate size of the tree. The shape of the apple tree is formed by the first three or four years' pruning. The first winter after budding or grafting, the tree is a single stick called a *maiden*.

The growth is cut back to 600 mm (a correct pruning cut is made, the uppermost bud will grow into the new leader) and the next year's growth produces a *feathered maiden*. After a third year of pruning an open-centred bush is produced with five main branches.

The maiden could have been pruned to form a dwarf pyramid:

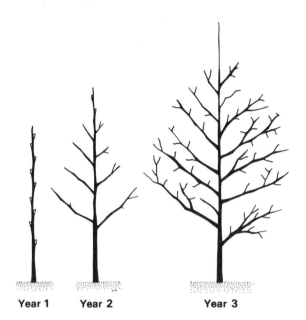

Year 1   Year 2   Year 3

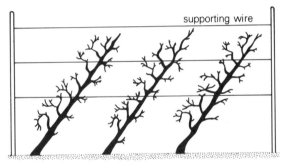

after pruning:
Year 1   Year 2   Year 3   Year 4

Other shapes of tree produced by tying and additional summer pruning include:

Cordon

Or the maiden could have been pruned to form a spindle bush, the branches being trained into a horizontal position by tying them down with strings attached to pegs in the ground:

Spindle tree being formed

Espallier

Cordons and espalliers are tied to horizontal wires, stretched between posts. All the trees above are small enough to allow operations to be carried out from the ground.

Apples are pruned each year after the basic shape of the tree has been established.

76 GCSE Rural Science 2

Aims of the apple pruner:
1. To encourage the main branches to follow the desired pattern.
2. To prevent overcrowding of branches and spurs.
3. To encourage the production of fruit buds.
4. To restrict the height and spread of the tree.
5. To allow sunlight to penetrate the centre of the tree.
6. To remove dead and diseased wood.

A correctly pruned tree will give a continuous supply of top quality fruit for many years. An unpruned tree will fruit before the pruned tree but the amount, size and quality of fruit will quickly decline. The pruner uses a knife, secateurs, long handled secateurs, long reach secateurs, and a variety of saws. If a saw is used the wound on the tree is painted over with bituminous paint to prevent disease organisms entering the wound. When pruning is completed the tools are sharpened and oiled and a little oil is smeared over unprotected parts before the tools are stored.

Why are the tools smeared with oil? ...Q.14

Varieties of apple
Selection of the varieties to be planted is of extreme importance. Most apple flowers are self-sterile and require the pollen from a *different variety* of apple tree for successful fertilisation. Unless the majority of the ten ovules the flower possesses are fertilised, a fruit will not develop.

What is the maximum number of pips an apple will have? ...Q.15

It is not possible to grow orchards of only one type of apple, as another variety must be present to provide the ncessary pollen for the fruit to set. The normal practice is to have every third row of trees of a pollinating variety:

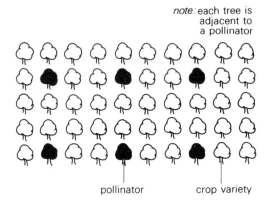

Pollination is further complicated by the fact that different varieties of apples flower at different times in the spring.

There are over 160 varieties of apples, the most important of which are: Cox's Orange Pippin, Golden Delicious, Worcester Pearmain, Egremont Russet, Bramley's Seedling, Grenadier and Lord Derby. The first four varieties are dessert apples and the other tree are cooking apples. The period during which most apples flower is divided into six parts, numbered 1 to 6.

Trees in group one flower first, and trees in group six flower last. During most seasons there is considerable overlapping, e.g. group 3 will be in flower before all group 2 flowers are dead, and some group 3 will be still open when group 4 begin to flower.

Flowering group	1	2	3	4	5	6
	Stark Earliest	Egremont Russet	Miller's Seedling	Grenadier	Lord Derby	Edward VII
		Lodi	James Grieve	Worcester Pearmain	Laxton's Superb	
		George Cave	Sunset	Golden Delicious	Ellison's Orange	
		Lord Lambourne	Beauty of Bath	Bramley's Seedling	Howgate Wonder	
			Merton Worcester			
			Fortune			
			Crispin			

If you wished to plant three apple trees, two of which were Egremont Russets, which variety ought you to choose for the third tree? ...Q.16

Pollinating insects

Apple blossom is insect pollinated. Bumble bees and other wild species of bees, together with the honey bee, are the insects mainly responsible for apple pollination. Fruit growers often hire hives of honey bees during blossom time to obtain a better set of fruit. Two or three hives to each hectare of orchard, set well away from the boundary, is the normal practice.

For what two reasons do bees visit apple flowers? ...Q.17

Planting a dormant apple tree

A hole is dug in the top soil wide enough to take the tree roots. A stout support post is driven into the bottom of the hole 100 mm to the side of the tree position. The tree is positioned and care taken that the graft union is above soil level and the tree approximately the same depth it was in the nursery.

The roots are carefully teased into position and covered with fine soil, which is then trodden down firmly.

The tree is secured to the stake with a tie designed to hold the tree some 75 mm from the stake to prevent chafing of the bark. The newly-planted tree must be protected, if necessary, from horses, cattle, sheep, goats, pigs, deer, rabbits, hares and voles.

How does a rabbit damage a tree? ...Q.18

Feeding the tree

Apples have a high requirement for nitrogen and potash and a low requirement for phosphate: 25 g/m^2 of complete fertilizer 6:3:15, or straight fertilisers applied in the same ratio, will meet the tree's requirements on most soils.

Too much nitrogen causes excessive tree growth and too much potash restricts the availability of another essential element – magnesium.

Some small fruitlets fall naturally from the tree in June – the June drop – and this thinning improves fruit quality. After the June drop use a pair of scissors to remove weak fruitlets where they appear overcrowded.

Apples ripen over a period and should be harvested as they ripen; fruit on the top of the tree is first to ripen and the shaded fruit in the middle of the tree ripens last. To test for ripeness, gently lift and twist: if the apple comes away easily it is ripe; the seeds inside the fruit should have turned brown.

Storing apples

Many of the late varieties of apples can be stored without special equipment for several months, the Bramley's Seedling, for example.

Perfect unblemished fruit individually wrapped in newspaper and placed on potato trays will keep in a cool moist atmosphere. Warm, dry environments or fluctuating temperatures are unsuitable for apple storage.

Growers have specially constructed apple stores where constant low temperatures are maintained. After they are gathered the apples continue to respire as part of the ripening process and once ripe the fruit deteriorates. In order to extend the keeping period the respiration rate of apples is reduced and this can be achieved by allowing the concentration of carbon dioxide to build up by restricted ventilation. The typical environment inside the apple store has a temperature of 3.5°C and an atmosphere that contains 8% carbon dioxide.

Assuming the nitrogen in the store's atmosphere remains constant (i.e. 80%), what is the percentage of oxygen when the percentage of carbon dioxide is eight? ...Q.19

Pests and diseases of apples

The apple crop is subject to a large number of pests and diseases and modern production methods would be impossible without a comprehensive spray programme. Mature orchards can require as much as 30 000 litres of water per hectare each year to mix the sprays. In winter, sprays of pesticides dissolved in tar oil are used on the leafless trees; the oil covers and penetrates places where water would just run off.

When the trees are in leaf pesticides are dissolved in water and the spraying equipment produces a cloud of very small water particles that reach otherwise inaccessible places.

Open blossom is never sprayed; why not? ...Q.20

Winter moths *(Operophtera brumata)*

The caterpillars of several species of moth feed on the leaves of apple trees during the spring. The loss of leaf reduces the amount of photosynthesis which, in turn, reduces the amount of substances which can be translocated to grow apples.

In bad attacks the tree can lose all its leaves; if this happens the tree grows new leaves but the crop is lost that year and seriously reduced the following year.

Larva of the winter moth

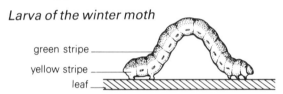

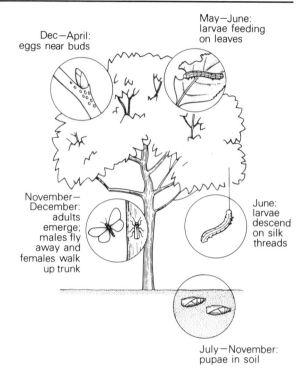

Life cycle of the winter moth

Caterpillars feed on leaves, buds and flowers; some spin a web to hold two leaves together, protecting themselves against birds whilst they feed.

Adults emerge in November and December from pupae in the soil. The females are wingless and crawl up the trunks of the trees; the brown, winged males fly freely and mate with the females.

On reaching the thinner branches and twigs the female lays about 200 eggs, placing them in bark crevices near to the buds.

In April, the larvae emerge from the eggs and at this stage they are so small that they may be blown from one tree to another. During the four to six week feeding period the larvae grow to lengths of 30 mm. When fully grown the larvae lower themselves towards the ground on silken threads they spin during the descent. On reaching the ground they burrow into the soil and change to pupae which will emerge as adults in November.

Control: Shrews and carabid beetles feed on pupae and some birds feed on the larvae. Robins collect larvae for their young. You can encourage robins with bird tables. Man reduces the numbers of winter moths in various ways.

Bands of paper, 150 mm wide, are tied around the trunks of trees one metre from the ground. The paper is covered with a liberal layer of

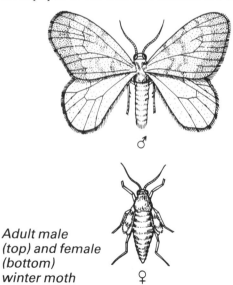

Adult male (top) and female (bottom) winter moth

grease in which the ascending females become stuck. The bands are inspected every two weeks to make sure that insects and dust have not formed a crust over which the moths can crawl.

Tar oil winter wash sprayed during frost-free days in winter kills some, but not all, of the eggs. Larvae are killed when they are small by spraying trees with trichlorphon.

Task 4.6

1. Obtain some twigs from an old neglected apple tree.
2. Examine carefully with a hand lens the areas around the buds and crevices in the bark. Note any evidence of insects, e.g. eggs, insect skeletons, and so on.
3. Cut off small pieces of the thinner twigs and examine under a low power microscope. Note the colour and shape of the insect eggs which may, or may not, be those of the winter moth.

Apple sawfly (Hoplocampa testudinea)
The larva of the sawfly tunnels under the skin of apple fruitlets leaving a visible scar across the fruit. It then turns towards the centre and feeds upon the developing seeds. The half-grown larva leaves the first fruit and enters a second, this time tunnelling directly to the seeds. The fruitlets, having lost their seeds, cease development and drop off the tree.

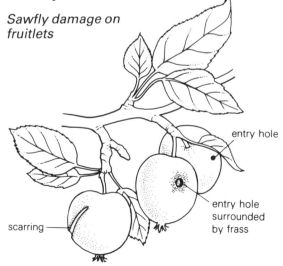

Sawfly damage on fruitlets

entry hole

entry hole surrounded by frass

scarring

Sawfly larvae have normally finished feeding by the end of June, when they drop on to the soil, burrow into it and enter a pre-pupal stage. In March, the pre-pupal stage ends and a pupa forms; four weeks later the adults emerge from the soil.

The adult female settles on the underside of an open apple flower and uses her saw-like ovipositor to cut into the receptacle and deposits an egg. During her eight day life the insect lays some thirty eggs, one to a flower. After an incubation period of five days, the larvae hatch and begin their journey through the fruitlet.

Control: Growers spray during the seven day period following petal fall with gamma-BHC, or other insecticides, to kill the emerging larvae. If spraying is delayed beyond seven days the larvae will have commenced tunnelling under the skin; they may be killed but the fruit will be scarred.

Earlier spraying will kill pollinating insects, as gamma-BHC is lethal to bees for 36 hours after spraying.

In gardens where there are few trees, effective control of sawfly can be achieved in June by picking off infested fruits – easily recognised by the tunnels under the skin – and burning them. Spraying with malathion or gamma-BHC may be carried out according to manufacturer's instructions but extreme care must be taken to protect pollinating insects and to prevent the drift of the spray to food crops. Bees are killed in unexpected ways, for example by spray falling on dandelions growing under the trees.

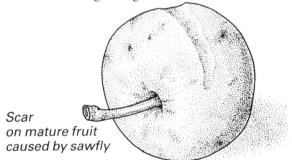

Scar on mature fruit caused by sawfly

The codling moth (Laspeyresia pomonella)
The larva of the codling moth burrows into immature fruit in a similar way to the sawfly larva; no scar is produced and codling moth larvae do not appear until the sawfly larvae have finished feeding.

80 GCSE Rural Science 2

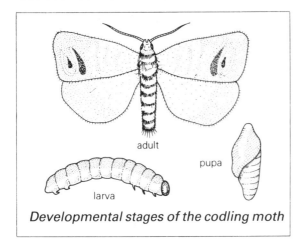

Developmental stages of the codling moth

The adults have a wing span of 20 mm. Wings are deep grey with wavy brown lines; the oval patches at the end are deep golden colour giving easy identification. During the day the moth rests on the branches and leaves of apple trees with wings folded to form a roof over the body. Like other moths it is active at night.

Larva of the codling moth in a mature fruit

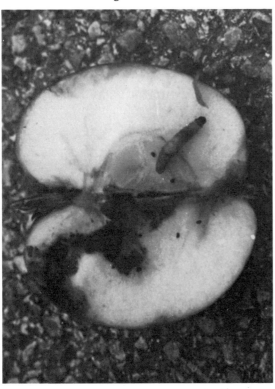

Task 4.7

During June make a careful search of the school apple trees for adult codling moths. Record any observations and make careful drawings.

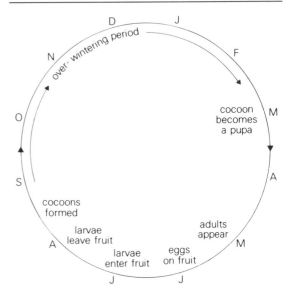

Life cycle of the codling moth

Moths appear at the end of May and lay 50–100 eggs singly on fruitlets when they are about 12 mm in diameter. Eggs are very small, oval and flat, more like a scale than an egg.

A week or so later, depending upon temperature, the eggs hatch. A newly-hatched larva begins feeding in the calyx and tunnels to the centre of the fruitlet to eat the seeds – pushing back into the tunnel its excrement and apple morsels, known as *frass*. The larva feeds for three or four weeks and leaves the apple through a hole in the skin. It crawls to a crevice in the bark, spins a cocoon of silk covered with a sticky fluid, and spends the winter inside. At the beginning of spring the larva pupates and a few weeks later the adult emerges.

Control: Growers spray insecticide in mid-June and again three weeks later, to control codling moth. Included in these sprays are substances to control red spider and apple scab.

In gardens, sections of the bark can be scraped fairly smooth and pieces of sacking and corrugated paper tied around the trunks and branches in June. Codling moth larvae make their cocoons in these traps which are removed and burned during the winter.

In schools they make excellent material for study. The sacking can be taken into the classroom for investigation and the cardboard left on the trees to make observations of birds feeding on the cocoons.

The female codling moth produces a pheromone (a smelly chemical) to attract its mate. The trap shown in the diagram has some of this chemical in the centre of a sticky platform. The males are attracted and get stuck in the sticky substance, leaving the females unfertilised. The use of these traps is an excellent method of controlling codling moths in a small garden, as no other creatures are harmed.

Task 4.8

Read the two accounts above on sawfly and codling moth. In summer pick up a fallen apple, cut it open and find an insect larva feeding inside. State TWO ways you could determine whether it was the larva of a sawfly or a codling moth. Turn to the end of the chapter and check your answer.

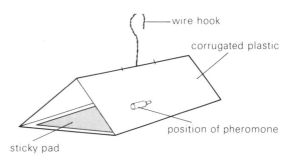

Questions: Fruit

1. Write single sentences to answer the following questions:
   (a) Name a soft fruit which produces runners.
   (b) Where does the shallot aphid overwinter?
   (c) What happens to a raspberry cane after fruiting?
   (d) What is a mulch?
   (e) How does the colour of blackcurrant wood vary with age?
   (f) What may extra large buds on some blackcurrant bushes contain?
   (g) Why are apple trees budded or grafted?
   (h) What does an apple stoolbed produce?
   (i) Why are the winter moths which are trapped by grease bands more likely to be female than male?
   (j) Why are the codling moths caught in pheromone traps more likely to be male than female?

2. (a) Name two forms of apple trees which are suitable for growing in the smaller garden.
   (b) Choose one of these forms and describe with words and diagrams how it can be produced from a maiden tree.

3. Draw a diagrammatic row of raspberries to show the situation at the end of harvest. Colour, or shade, the canes which are more than one year old.
   Draw a second diagram showing the same row after pruning.

4. (a) Describe the life cycle of the winter moth.
   (b) List the moth's natural predators in a vertical column and alongside each state in which part of the life cycle the predation occurs.
   (c) In what ways are non-chemical methods

of codling moth control better than chemical ones?

5. With words and diagrams describe the following:
   (a) Propagation of blackcurrants from hardwood cuttings.
   (b) Propagation of strawberries from runners.
   (c) Grafting an apple scion on to a rootstock.
   (d) Why is it better to grow fruit trees by the methods you have described rather than from seed?

6. (a) With words and diagrams describe how a bud of Cox's Orange Pippin is made to grow on a an M26 rootstock (refer to budding roses, Chapter 5).
   (b) Would the tree which results from the above operation be suitable to train as a cordon? Give reasons for your answer.

7. The four apple trees in an isolated garden had very poor crops. When the owner bought a fifth tree the original four began to have heavy yields.
   (a) Explain why the yields of the trees increased.
   (b) What can you deduce about the variety of the new tree?
   (c) What other steps could the owner take to increase the yields of his trees?
   (d) Explain why spraying apples against sawfly can reduce yields.

8. Extract from *The Fruit Growers' Companion*:

   The blackcurrant is propagated from hardwood cuttings; these are grown on for a year and then planted in the final positions some 15 cm deeper than they were in the nursery bed. Perennial weeds are extremely troublesome as, due to the bush having green buds, sprays are not very selective. Annual weeds are easily controlled with a deep mulch of organic matter.

   (a) Explain the following terms: propagated; hardwood; perennial; selective; annual; mulch.
   (b) Why are blackcurrant bushes planted 15 cm deeper when moved to their final positions?
   (c) Black polythene can also be used as a mulch to control weeds. What are the advantages and disadvantages of using black polythene instead of organic matter for mulching soft fruit?

9. A grower took two days to straw a field of strawberries. During the intervening night there was a late spring frost. This frost considerably reduced the yield of the part which had been strawed but had no effect on the unstrawed part.
   (a) Why are strawberries 'strawed'?
   (b) Use words and diagrams to explain why one section of the field was affected by frost and not the other.
   (c) Strawberries survive frost and snow throughout the winter and yet spring frosts cause damage. Explain why this is so.

5 Gardens

Flowers

Chrysanthemum *(Chrysanthemum morifolium)*

Chrysanthemums have been cultivated in China since before 500 BC.

They were introduced to Europe at the end of the eighteenth century and are now the second most important commercial flower in Britain.

Chrysanthemums are also widely grown in private gardens as both border plants and cut flowers.

Which is the most important commercial flower?
...Q.1

Project 5.1
To produce a crop of chrysanthemums

This project spans two academic years and should begin before the final year in school.

Part A
(To run concurrently with part C)

1. In January obtain a number of chrysanthemum stools of an early flowering variety:

A box of chrysanthemum stools

2. Plant the stools fairly close together in a plant tray of John Innes potting compost.
3. Water well and leave in a warm, light place.
4. Early in March the stools will be covered in shoots. Select ten strong shoots and remove them with a sharp knife.
5. Prepare the shoots into cuttings by cutting off the bottom just below a node, leaving the shoot about 60 mm long. Remove the two or three bottom leaves. If the remaining shoot is leafy reduce the size of two of the leaves by cutting in half.

Why is the leaf area of the cutting reduced?
...Q.2

6. Fill a 225 mm pot with a mixture of equal parts peat and sharp sand. Water well.
7. Dip the bottom 10 mm of each cutting in a rooting powder and insert them to leave about half the cutting above the compost. Space the cuttings as far apart as possible but keep them well away from the edge of the pot.
8. Cover with a ploche and place in a warm light place but *not* in direct sunlight.
9. After one week open the vents on the ploche.

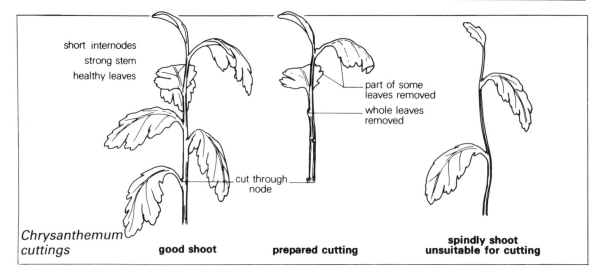

Chrysanthemum cuttings — good shoot — prepared cutting — spindly shoot unsuitable for cutting

Part B

1. Three or four weeks after taking the cuttings, gently pull at one. If it feels firmly attached to the rooting medium it has rooted; if it tends to lift easily it has not.
2. When the cuttings have rooted lift them carefully and pot individually in 75 mm pots of John Innes No. 3 potting compost.
3. Grow on in a greenhouse or classroom window for two weeks, then transfer the plants in their pots to a cold frame.
4. Harden off by giving a little more air every few days. By the end of May the lights should be completely removed. This timing will vary according to local climatic conditions; chrysanthemums that are properly hardened off will not be harmed by frost.

Part C

(*This part of the task runs concurrently with parts A and B*)

1. In common with most other crops chrysanthemums will not tolerate waterlogged soil. Select a site where the drainage is good and dig, working the soil two spits deep, adding compost or farmyard manure.
2. Before the end of the autumn term, test the pH of the soil and if it is 6 or below, spread 50 g/m^2 of ground limestone or chalk over the soil surface.
3. During April spread 20 g/m^2 of 10:15:5 complete fertiliser over the soil and rake down to form a tilth.
4. Chrysanthemums have a high magnesium requirement; 20 g/m^2 of magnesium sulphate (Epsom salts) added to light soils will correct any deficiency in this element.

Part D

1. Towards the end of May, when soil conditions are suitable, tap the plants from their pots.

What soil conditions will be suitable? ...Q.3

2. Taking care not to disturb the soil balls, plant with a trowel in rows 400 mm apart and 400 mm between the plants. After every fourth row leave a space of one metre to form a path.
3. Pinch out the growing point from each plant (this is called stopping the plant):

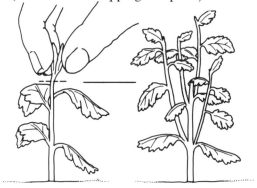

pinch out growing point — buds grow from the nodes

4. Drive one stake into each corner of the four row bed. If the rows are over six metres long, intermediate posts will be required along the sides of the bed.
5. Stretch a plastic garden net (100 mm squares) horizontally between the four posts above the plants at a height of 350 mm and a second net at a height of 650 mm. Support the four sides of each net with tomato twine tied to the posts and woven along the edge of the net. The flowers will grow through the net which will give them all the support they require:

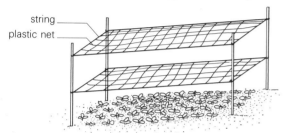

Note: if only a few plants are to be grown, push a 1250 mm cane into the soil to a depth of 420 mm close to the stem of each plant. Tie each flower stem loosely to the stake; second and even third ties will be required as the plants grow.

6. Keep the soil between the rows weed-free by dutch hoeing and hand weeding.

Part E

1. Four or five main stems will grow up from each plant. At the beginning of June and again just before the end of the summer term 'disbud' each stem by removing all the buds at the nodes except the topmost bud. Disbudding increases the size of the flower and the length of the stem.
2. Ideally the plants should be disbudded several times from mid-August to mid-September.
3. A few weeks later you will be rewarded with a crop of beautiful, long stemmed chrysanthemums which, if cut, will keep in water for over two weeks.

A chrysanthemum plant which has not been disbudded

A chrysanthemum plant which has been disbudded

Late flowering chrysanthemums

Late flowering chrysanthemums are varieties which bloom in the greenhouse during November, December and January. They are grown in a similar way to early chrysanthemums except they are planted either into 300 mm pots or adjacent to a mobile greenhouse.

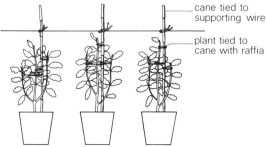

cane tied to supporting wire

plant tied to cane with raffia

During October the pots are taken into the greenhouse or the mobile greenhouse is rolled over the plants; the most likely crop to precede late flowering chrysanthemums in the greenhouse is tomatoes.

Photoperiodism

The time of flowering of many plants is governed by the length of the day.

1. Long day plants flower readily when the days are long and will not flower when the days are short. Examples: radish, spinach, godetia and lettuce.
2. Short day plants flower when the nights are longer than the days, for example Michaelmas daisy, strawberry, cosmos, and tobacco.
3. Day-neutral plants are plants with flowering periods unaffected by day length and will flower under any lighting conditions, providing they receive sufficient light for photosynthesis, for example: dandelion, cucumber, tomato and hydrangea.

Chrysanthemums belong to group two – the short day plants. For this reason it is not possible to flower early chrysanthemums outside much before August. Growers of greenhouse chrysanthemums artificially control the day-length to induce their chrysanthemums to flower at any time of year; e.g. in time for Mother's Day.

To achieve short days and long nights the greenhouses are fitted with black polythene blinds which are pulled down early in the evening and left in position until well after daybreak. The plants respond to this treatment by producing flowers in seasons where, under natural lighting conditions, they would make only vegetative growth. Production of out-of-season chrysanthemums has become a large industry. In addition to controlling the flowering periods, growers also use plant hormones to reduce the height of the plants.

Pests of chrysanthemums

Many creatures find the chrysanthemum good to eat: aphids, red spiders, larvae of various moths, eelworms and leaf miner. Well-grown plants from healthy stock will provide food for some of these pests in addition to a crop of flowers. This is especially true in gardens where the use of pesticides is kept to an absolute minimum and healthy populations of natural predators exist. In such gardens ladybirds and their larvae are a common sight during disbudding.

What pest does the ladybird feed upon?...Q.4

Leaf miner

Investigation 5.1

(September is the best time for this investigation.)

1. Examine the photograph (below, opposite) and note the damage to the leaf.
2. Go outside and collect a number of leaves which show similar damage (chrysanthemum, celery, poplar tree, fathen, sow thistle and many other plants can be found with this type of damage).
3. Using two dissecting pins and a hand lens investigate the leaves and answer the questions below.

(a) Does the mark on the leaf follow any regular pattern? ...Q.5
(b) Is the mark continuous, or are there a lot of small marks? ...Q.6
(c) Is the mark exactly the same width throughout its length? ...Q.7
(d) Examine both ends of the mark; what can be seen? ...Q.8
(e) Remembering the internal structure of the leaf, examine the mark and say which parts of the leaf are missing and which parts are intact. ...Q.9
(f) Use the dissecting pins to remove the creature from the end of a short mark; examine carefully. What kind of creature is it? ...Q.10
(g) Remove a creature from the end of a long mark that is widened at the end. Examine; what kind of creature is this? ...Q.11
(h) List three advantages the creature has from living inside the leaf. ...Q.12

4. Use an insect cage and a number of infested leaves to obtain the adult form.

By comparison with the housefly would you expect the adult to be large or small? ...Q.13

5. Record the investigation (including diagrams).

The insect you have just investigated was the leaf miner; the actual species depends upon the plant upon which it was found. The chrysanthemum leaf miner is *Phytomza syngenesiae*.

The adult miner is similar in appearance to a house fly except that it has a wing span of only 4 mm and is grey in colour. The adult lays its eggs in slits cut on the undersurface of the leaf and moves in a series of short hopping flights from one leaf to another. Adult females also pierce the leaves with their ovipositors in order to obtain the sap on which they feed. Feeding marks on the leaves appear as small, light coloured spots. Chrysanthemums grown under glass are often badly infested; the loss of photosynthetic tissue causes the death of young plants and reduction of flowering in older plants.

Life cycle:
In the artificial environment of the heated greenhouse six or more generations of leaf miner are possible in one year. The egg hatches into a small larva which begins tunnelling as it feeds.

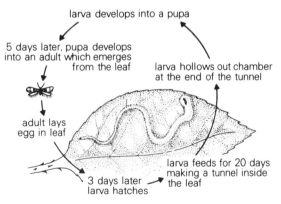

Life cycle of the leaf miner

The initial tunnel is small but increases in diameter as the larva grows. When fully grown (4 mm long) the larva eats a chamber in the spongy tissue of the leaf and pupates, and a few days later the adult emerges. Under glass, the time from egg to adult varies from 20 to 28 days according to temperature. Control in greenhouses is by three applications of gamma-BHC smoke or spray at ten day intervals.

Out of doors there are two generations of this leaf miner and little damage is caused. The insect overwinters as a pupa.

How could some control be achieved out of doors without the use of chemicals? ...Q.14

Chrysanthemum eelworm (Aphelenchoides ritzemabosi)
This eelworm, which can also live upon over 100 other plants and weeds, is probably the most troublesome pest of chrysanthemums. Infected plants develop yellow/green patches between the veins of the lower leaves. These patches turn brown and spread over the leaf which then falls. The condition gradually moves up the plant as the eelworms climb higher.

Life cycle: If the eelworm is present in the base of the plant and swims up the stems when they are wet, the female deposits her eggs on undamaged leaves, they hatch in one to three days and larvae are fully grown ten days later.

Feeding: The eelworms enter the leaves through the stomata and feed on the internal tissues of the leaf.

Why is it possible for such a small nematode to cause such a large amount of damage? ...Q.15

Nematodes in fallen leaves coil up and remain dormant until they are wetted, when normal activity resumes.

Control: Infected stools produce infected cuttings. The old method of inserting stools in hot water (which kills the eelworms and not the plants) is now little used as temperatures and timings have to be very precise.

Infected cuttings, grown quickly in heat, have their tips removed when they are 250 mm high. The tips are rooted and grown as quickly as possible to a height of 250 mm. Cuttings taken from the tips of these will be free from eelworm as they grew more quickly than the eelworms could climb.

The school gardener can protect the plants against eelworm by smearing petroleum jelly around the base of the stems, to prevent the eelworms from climbing to the leaves. The petroleum jelly has to be renewed as the stems increase in girth.

Chemical control is achieved by soaking the rooted cuttings and soil with thionazin solution which is taken up by the roots; two dressings are given at 12 day intervals.

Outside, good hygiene will result in reduced risk of infection; plant refuse and dead infected leaves must be burnt. The ground upon which infected plants grew must be kept weed free throughout the winter to prevent eelworms overwintering on weeds.

Rose (hybrids of *Rosa indica* and *R. damascena* on the roots of *R. canina*)

The above botanical names are an over-simplification; in fact many closely related species of *rosa* have been combined to obtain the wide range of desirable characteristics found in the modern rose. Hybridisation has produced thousands of varieties, dozens of colours, and five different flower types. The flowering period of most types has also been extended to almost six months from June to November.

Hybrid Tea
Bred in France in 1860 the hybrid tea (H.T.) rose has a few large double flowers on each stalk.

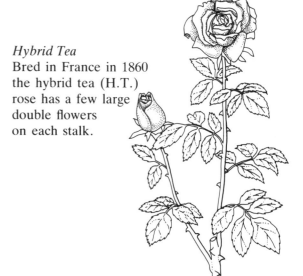

Floribunda
Bred in Denmark in 1924, the floribunda rose has clusters of small flowers on each stalk with many open at the same time.

The rose is a perennial bush or shrub which does not mix well with other flowers and is best grown in beds devoted entirely to roses.

Plant forms include:

Propagation

Roses grown from seed are not true to type; plants from cuttings, although true to type, grow into unsatisfactory bushes. Nearly all roses are therefore grown on rootstocks by budding.

Rootstocks
The wild dog rose (*Rosa canina*) is the most popular rootstock; it is easy to propagate and produces a vigorous bush that withstands transplanting.

Rosa multiflora is sometimes used as a rootstock for roses that are to be grown on light soils; roses grown on this rootstock do not live as long as those grown on *Rosa canina*.

Rosa rugosa is often used for standards. (A standard is produced by inserting two buds, one metre up the stem of the rootstock.) This rootstock produces many suckers and is unsuitable for bush roses.

Rosa laxa is almost thornless and easy to bud.

Task 5.1

A sucker growing from the ground by a rose bush is rootstock material. Collect a sucker and a piece of the rose bush. Compare the leaves, stems and thorns and write an account of their differences.

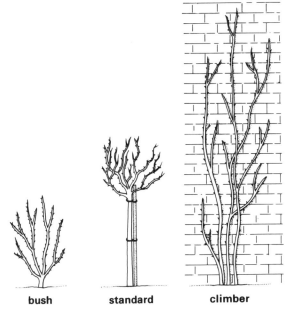

bush   standard   climber

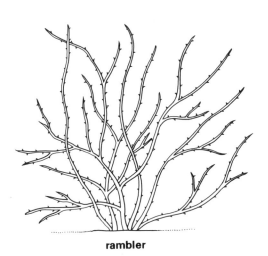

rambler

Budding

Budding is the grafting of a single bud of a scion to a rootstock. The aerial parts of the resulting plant all grow from the scion bud.

Task 5.2

(June is the best time for this task.)

1. Obtain a length of stem from a wild rose about 200 mm long.
2. Clamp the stem upright in a retort stand.
3. Make a T-shaped cut through the rind down to the wood using a very sharp knife or scalpel. Gently ease the bark away from the wood at A and B:
4. Using the stem of a garden rose as scion material, select a good bud and, beginning 10 mm below, cut underneath the bud. Curve the cut upwards to a point about 10 mm above the bud; on reaching this point tear upwards to leave a strip of rind to form a handle:

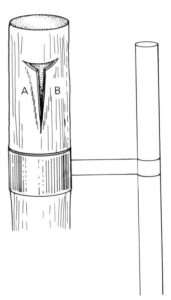

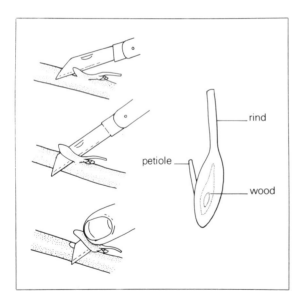

During this operation cut *away* from the hand that is holding the stem.

5. Carefully remove the small piece of wood from the back of the bud.
6. Slide the bud shield behind flaps A and B on the stock.

7. Cut off the protruding portion of the rind C and tie with raffia:

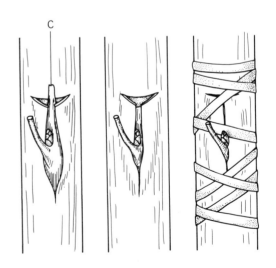

8. Remove raffia after two weeks.

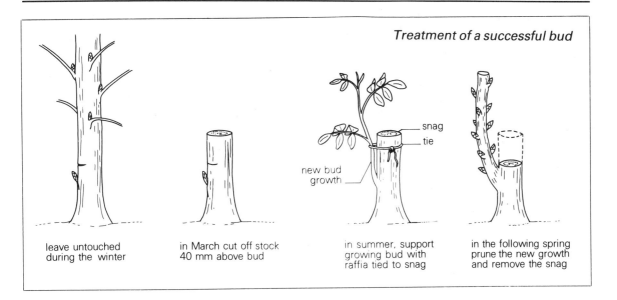

Treatment of a successful bud

leave untouched during the winter | in March cut off stock 40 mm above bud | in summer, support growing bud with raffia tied to snag | in the following spring prune the new growth and remove the snag

Today commercial growers use a strip of rubber 25 mm wide which clips around the stock holding the bud in position. Unlike raffia, the rubber clip does not have to be removed after two weeks as it stretches with the girth and later perishes.

In the autumn, if the bud has united with the stock, the petiole under the bud will drop off naturally. If the budding has failed the petiole will wither and the bud will die.

Bush roses are budded near to the ground. Standard roses have two buds inserted, one metre or so from the ground.

Growing roses

Site
A site in the open garden, sheltered from cold winds, where there is little or no shade is ideal for bush roses.

Soil
Roses thrive on clay soils, providing they do not become waterlogged, and are well supplied with humus. Clay soil is not essential, as most loams grow good roses, especially if the pH is below 6.5. They are difficult to grow on calcareous soils. All soils should be deeply worked, given a heavy dressing of compost or farmyard manure and be free from perennial weeds. A hole broad enough to allow the roots to spread is dug to a depth that will just cover the union between the stock and scion:

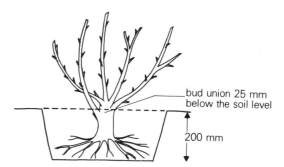

Carefully arrange the roots in the hole, half fill with soil and gently firm with the sole of the foot. Fill the hole and tread firmly before raking the surface to a tidy finish.

In March, when there is no frost, prune the newly-planted bush to leave four or five buds on each stem with the uppermost bud on the outside of the bush.

Care of roses
In addition to annual pruning, roses must be kept free from weeds by light hoeing. A small feed of 30 g/m^2 of complete fertiliser given in spring followed by a mulch of well rotted compost will provide sufficient nutrients on most soils.

Dead flowers should be removed with a short length of stem, cutting always to an outward facing bud.

Why cut to an outward facing bud? ...Q.16

Pests and diseases of roses

Rose aphid
By far the most common pest of roses is the rose aphid (*Macrosiphum rosae*) which feeds by thrusting its proboscis into the plant, pumping in digestive juices and then sucking up the sap. The removal of sap from the plant affects its vigour, cripples the shoots, injures the buds and disfigures the foliage.

Control is by contact insecticides (derris or malathion) or by systemic insecticide.

Systemic insecticides are absorbed by the plants and translocated within them. Systemic insecticides are not washed off by rain and the sucking insect takes poison with its food.

Froghopper (Philaenus spumarius)
Froghoppers are small (6 mm long) active insects with well-developed legs enabling them to jump long distances. The adults suck the sap of a large range of plants and do little damage. The nymphs, however, select one feeding spot and remain there protected by a mass of spittle-like foam which gives them the name 'cuckoo-spit'. Affected shoots become distorted and leaves above the nymphs often wilt. Control by hand removal is sufficient for most gardens. Where a considerable number of bushes are affected, spray with insecticide in a jet which penetrates the foam to destroy the nymphs.

What is nymph? ...Q.17

Suggest another method of froghopper control. ...Q.18

Task 5.3

1. Search for 'cuckoo-spit', but do not confine your search to roses. Look on other plants, e.g. lavender, campanula, phlox and geum.
2. Remove the foam complete with the nymph.
3. Examine the nymph using a magnifying glass and make a drawing of it.

Suggest two ways the nymph benefits from the foam. ...Q.19

Fungal diseases
The most serious diseases of the rose are caused by parasitic fungi and include mildew, black spot and rust.

Name a group of food plants that are also affected by rust diseases. ...Q.20

Control: Spray or dust with a fungicide (marathane/dithane mixture) at two-weekly intervals when the first signs of the diseases are noticed. Burn any infected material which falls, or is pruned off.

Note: It was thought that the heavy pollution around towns and cities from smokey fires used to control black spot on roses. Since the Clean Air Acts some of the pollutants have been reduced. This may be the cause of increased black spot on roses in city gardens. There is, however, some doubt about this as smokeless fuels still contain a percentage of sulphur which enters the atmosphere as the fuel is burned.

Garden design

Home gardens may contain some or all of these: (1) Lawn; (2) Trees; (3) Shrubs; (4) Herbaceous perennials; (5) Biennials – flowers; (6) Annuals – flowers; (7) Vegetables; (8) Hedges; (9) Paths; (10) Fences; (11) Rocks; (12) Water; (13) Structures to give height e.g. trellis; (14) Items such as bird tables and baths, garden ornaments etc.; (15) Greenhouse; (16) Garden shed; (17) A clothes-drying area.

By *garden design* we mean the way in which the above items are arranged to look attractive and meet the family's needs. A family with very young children would probably require a large lawn and no water, as garden pools can be very dangerous for toddlers. A family with old or disabled members would require wide paths with ramps rather than steps; if they liked gardening then raised beds could be included in the design. If the family had a very keen cook then herbs could be included. These should be near to the kitchen door and within easy reach of the path. A garden with a small lawn surrounded by large shrubs would suit the family with little time for gardening. The diagrams show the same garden designed in four different ways.

A garden showing use of curves and plants of various heights – small at the front, large at the back

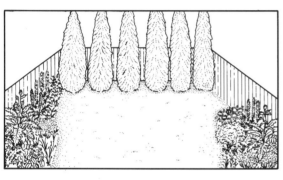

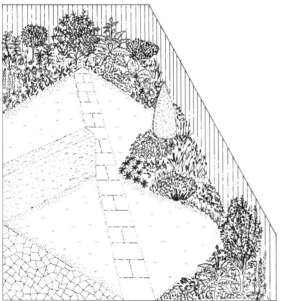

Task 5.4

1. Examine the designs on page 93 and say which, in your opinion is: (a) the worst and (b) the best, giving reasons for your choices.
2. Design a garden for a family where the father can grow vegetables, the mother can grow flowers, the son can raise pot plants in a greenhouse and the daughter can sunbathe in privacy. (Remember that straight lines should be avoided where possible in a flower garden but they are quite acceptable in a vegetable garden.)

Take your table and a quadrat to an area of lawn. Examine the lawn carefully and complete the table e.g. a very bumpy lawn would score 0 and a fairly flat one would score 3.

Using your quadrat make a number of random throws, each time counting the number of weeds present. Divide the total number of weeds by the number of throws to obtain an average. Subtract your average from 9 to give a score (ignore negative values). Add this score to the total mark from your chart. This final total will be a mark out of 25. Repeat this task on other lawns and compare the results.

Lawns

Lawns are grassed areas which are kept short by regular cutting. They have many uses in addition to being ornamental. Different uses require different species of grass; playing football on a bowling green, for example, would prove disastrous. What all grassed areas have in common is that they must be well drained and well maintained.

Very few gardens are without a lawn yet a good lawn is one of the most difficult things to achieve. A good lawn is an area of very short grass which contains no bumps or weeds. It is the same green colour all over and has no bare patches. Very few lawns are like this. There are probably a number of lawns around your school, let us take a look at them.

Grass species suitable for lawns
1. *Ornamental lawn.*
   (a) *Browntop (Agrostis tenuis):* very common lawn grass, produces short runners; a permanent grass which can withstand drought.
   (b) *Creeping bent (Agrotstis stolonifera):* has longer runners than browntop and therefore spreads more quickly; cannot withstand hard wear.
   (c) *Chewings fescue (Festuca rubra):* grows in tufts, is dark green and often included in luxury mixtures.
   (d) *Creeping red fescue (Festuca rubra gernuina).* A popular species for fine lawns, its advantage over chewings fescue is that it produces rhizomes and therefore spreads naturally.
2. *General purpose lawn.*
   (a) *Perennial ryegrass (Lolium perenne):* a very hard wearing grass which does not withstand close mowing.
   (b) *Annual meadow grass (Poa annua):* an indigenous grass which appears in all lawns. Regarded as a weed in top quality lawns, but useful as it will form a turf in poor light conditions (under trees) where other grasses would not survive.
   (c) *Crested dog's tail (Cunosurus cristatus):* grows in tufts. Very hard wearing and drought resistant.

Task 5.5

Copy the following table.

Score	Very 0	Fairly 1	In between 2	Fairly 3	Very 4
bumpy					flat
brown					green
long					short
mossy					little moss

Project 5.2

(This project is best carried out during April and May.)

Leave a small area of a lawn uncut and allow the grass to flower. Collect one of each type of flower, together with stalk and at least one leaf. Using this material and a 'key' from a reference book identify each type of grass in the lawn.

Maintaining a lawn

It is important to remember that a lawn is a crop and has similar requirements to other crops; it needs a good well-drained soil, containing plenty of air, water and a supply of all the elements needed for plant growth. Unlike many crop plants, however, lawns are better grown on a rather acid soil – pH 5 is suitable.

The crop plants (i.e. lawn grasses) need to be kept free from weeds; this is most easily achieved by the use of a selective herbicide like MCPA.

In addition to looking after the requirements of the plants lawns need regular cutting and edging.

Tools for lawn care

Task 5.6

Examine the tools below and, remembering the requirements of a lawn, say how and why each is used.

Investigation 5.2
To find the mass of nutrients removed from the soil by a lawn in a given period

1. Measure the area of a lawn in square metres.
2. Cut the lawn.
3. Two weeks later cut the lawn again using the same mower on the same settings.
4. Weigh the lawn mowings.
5. Calculate the weight produced by 1 m².
6. Weigh 500 g of cuttings and place in an oven set at 100°C until dry.
7. Burn the cuttings in a crucible until just the ash remains.
8. Weigh the ash on a very accurate balance.
9. Calculate the weight of ash 1 m² of lawn produced. (The ash is the minerals which the lawn removed from the soil.)

The material burnt off was carbohydrate. From where did the lawn grass obtain its carbohydrate?   ...Q.21

The use of rocks in garden design

When rocks are used they should be set in such a way as to make a natural feature. The individual stones should be set so they slope backwards. This prevents plants in front from being dripped on and lets water run back and water plants behind. If heathers are to be planted the soil between the stones should have a low pH, or use an ericaceous (i.e. low pH) compost.

This untidy hedge bottom was transformed with sandstone blocks set to look like a rock outcrop

Garden ponds

Look at the following pool shapes, which all have similar surface areas.

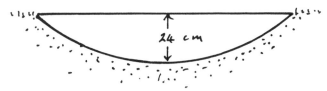

This pool holds about half as much water as the one below; it will warm and cool too quickly for pond life.

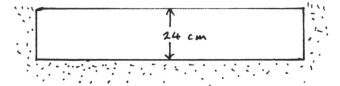

This will probably crack when the water freezes.

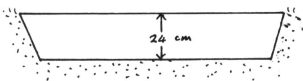

A pool with a 20° slope is less likely to crack.

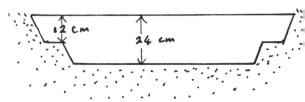

This pool has a shelf for plants which require shallow water. (Some pools have several shelves for plants requiring different water depths.)

It is important that the first plants to be introduced into a pool are those which grow completely submerged. These plants oxygenate the water and help to maintain a natural balance.

A garden pond in a sunny position

Questions: Gardens

1. Write single sentences to answer the following questions:

   (a) What is a lawn?
   (b) Explain the term 'herbaceous' when applied to a garden plant.
   (c) Why must a garden pool not have a large surface area:volume ratio?
   (d) Which insect causes white lines to appear in chrysanthemum leaves?
   (e) What use does a rose grower make of the species *Rosa canina*?
   (f) What environmental condition causes chrysanthemums to flower?
   (g) Why must rocks slope backwards in a rockery?
   (h) Which insect larva lives in 'cuckoo spit'?
   (i) Disbudding reduces the number of flowers a chrysanthemum produces; why is it done?

2. (a) How do growers carry over their stocks of decorative chrysanthemums from one year to the next?
   (b) How are chrysanthemum cuttings taken and prepared?
   (c) How are prepared cuttings given the conditions necessary for rooting?
   (d) Cuttings are rooted two months before being planted into their flowering positions. What treatments do they have at this time?
   (e) Why are chrysanthemums propagated vegetatively?

3. A house has a rear garden 8 metres wide and 30 metres long surrounded by a wooden fence 1.5 metres high. Design a garden with a lawn, pool, greenhouse, small shed, rockery, standard cherry tree, 12 different shrubs and a few herbs.

4. (a) What is a good lawn?
   (b) Why would a family with three children under six years old require a lawn?
   (c) What care would such a lawn require over a year?
   (d) Which grass species is most suitable for this lawn?
   (e) Worm casts are a problem on bowling greens and worm killers are used. Some householders do not mind worm casts and take no steps to eliminate worms from their lawns. In what ways are earthworms beneficial to (i) lawns and (ii) wildlife?

5. (a) How would you plant a new bare-root rose you bought? Include at least one diagram in your answer.
   (b) What are the advantages of roses grown in containers? State a disadvantage of container-grown roses.
   (c) Budding cannot be used to produce a new rose variety. Why not?

6. (a) Draw a large diagram to show a correct pruning cut.
   (b) Explain why the cut should be made in this way and the problems that incorrect pruning cuts can cause.

6 Sheep

Little is known about the ancestors of the modern sheep (*Ovis musimon*) which has probably been bred from a large number of closely-related wild species from Asia and Eastern Europe.

With a sheep population of 30 million, the United Kingdom has more sheep per hectare than any country except New Zealand. In contrast with New Zealand's four breeds, the UK has over thirty distinct breeds. The native sheep in many parts of the world have been improved by introducing blood from British breeds.

Sheep products

In the UK sheep are kept primarily for their meat which is known as lamb from a young animal and mutton from an older animal. The fleece and gut of a sheep are heavy and this reduces the killing out percentage to less than half the weight of the live animal.

Joints of lamb

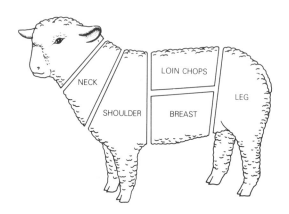

A shepherd has a 50 kg lamb slaughtered for his deep freeze; if the killing out percentage is 48 what weight will the shepherd place in his freezer? ...Q.1

Wool is an important by-product of sheep farming. In June or July (depending upon district and weather conditions), all sheep over one year old are sheared.

Shearing a sheep

The short-woolled breeds each produce about 1.5 kg of wool and the long-woolled breeds yield 5 kg or more.

Wool is the most important animal fibre and is used to make knitting wool, worsted cloth, carpets, tapestries and blankets.

Task 6.1

1. Obtain samples of wool from different breeds of sheep from the British Wood Marketing Board*.
2. Tease some fibres from each and place in separate piles.
3. Use a ruler and determine the average length of fibre in each pile.
4. Examine fibres from each of the three piles with a low power microscope, and look for
   (a) Uniformity of cross-section. Wool grown during a period of malnutrition has weak points known as 'breaks'.
   (b) Compare the fineness of the fibres from the three different sources. Fine fibres give the cloth a softness and better appearance.
   (c) Crimp, or waviness, which helps the fibres to cling together when spun. Fine Merino has waves only 1 mm long whilst the waves of long wools may be 6 mm long. Crimp gives springiness and elasticity to the finished cloth.
   (d) The appearance of the surface of the fibres; are they smooth or ridged?

Which would make the stronger material, a smooth fibre or a ridged fibre? ...Q.2

5. On completion of the examination make a copy of the chart below and complete it.

	Longwool	*Shortwool*	*Down*
Average length of fibres			
Uniformity of cross section			
Thickness			
Length of waves			
Appearance of surface			

*British Wool Marketing Board, Oak Mills, Station Road, Clayton, Bradford, West Yorkshire, B14 6JD

Another important quality of wool is its colour. White wool is easily dyed to the required colour; black and brown wools are difficult: it is for this reason that black sheep are unpopular with shepherds and seldom used for breeding.

Breeds of sheep

The many breeds of sheep can be divided into four groups; these groups often overlap, however, and new breeds are being imported (e.g. the Texel from France):

Mountain and moorland breeds

Derbyshire Gritstone
Shetland
Herdwick
Welsh Mountain
Whitefaced Dartmoor
Lonk
Rough Fell
Scottish Blackface
Swaledale

Hill breeds

Cheviot
Clun Forest
Kerry Hill
Radnor Forest

Short-woolled breeds

Dorset Horn
Wiltshire
Ryeland
Devon Closewool
Southdown
Shropshire
Suffolk
Dorset Down
Hampshire Down
Oxford Down

Long-woolled breeds

Devon Longwool
Border Leicester
Lincoln Longwool
Wensleydale
Romney Marsh
Improved Dartmoor

Mountain and moorland breeds are small (32–36 kg liveweight), active and hardy, their shoulders are rather narrow compared with other breeds and they mature more slowly.
Long-woolled breeds are large in size (60–75 kg liveweight) with rather broad backs; they have white faces and legs and are hornless. Long-woolled breeds are kept on fertile, lowland farms.
Short-woolled breeds of sheep are of intermediate size (45–55 kg liveweight) and are suited to

Scottish Blackface

Border Leicester cross Scottish Blackface

Down rams

lighter drier types of soils; they 'fold' well on arable crops. Down breeds have dark faces and legs and are hornless.

Hill breeds are medium-sized (45–55 kg liveweight), more hardy than the short- and long-woolled breeds, and larger and less hardy than the mountain and moorland breeds.

The Scottish Blackface is the most numerous breed in the UK. It thrives on the heather-clad moors in Scotland and Northern England. Flocks are also to be found on the moors of the South West peninsula. The breed is small but hardy and withstands much snow and heavy rain. The wool is most suitable for carpet manufacture and the meat is of high quality.

The Suffolk was bred in East Anglia for arable farm conditions. It is much used for cross-breeding with smaller types of ewes to give larger lambs. Lack of wool on the face makes lambing easier. The breed is quick to mature and prolific, giving a high proportion of twins.

In addition to the large variety of breeds listed above many shepherds keep first crosses – 'half-breds' – and mate them to a larger breed of ram (♂) to obtain better sized lambs.

Other breeds are still being developed; recently Mr Oscar Colburn developed 'Colbred' sheep from Border Leicester, Clun Forest, Dorset Horn and a foreign breed, East Friesland. Ewes (♀) of this breed nearly always produce twin lambs and give a high yield of milk.

What advantage is a high milk yield? ...Q.3

Colbred

Task 6.2

The varied climate and environments in Britain have given rise to a large number of different breeds of sheep.

Use an atlas, or your knowledge of the geography of your country, and pair the numbered breeds with the letters on the map:

1. Suffolk
2. Welsh Mountain
3. Dorset Horn
4. Romney (Kent)
5. Scotch Blackface
6. Dartmoor
7. South Down
8. Swaledale (just north Bradford)
9. Derbyshire Gritstone
10. Radnor
11. Wensleydale
12. North Country Cheviot (most northerly)
13. Cheviot
14. Herdwick (Lakes)
15. Shropshire
16. Oxford Down
17. Devon Longwool
18. Lincoln Longwool
19. Clun Forest (English/Welsh border)
20. Border Leicester (English/Scottish border)

Housing and handling

On most farms sheep live outside throughout the year, and when the level of nutrition in the herbage available is low they lose body weight by burning up their fat reserves to keep warm in cold weather.

To enable the shepherd to look after greater numbers of sheep and prevent loss of body weight and poaching of soils many experiments in sheep housing are being carried out. Flocks are being housed throughout the winter on slatted floors, in straw yards and part covered pens.

Many sheep that winter outside are partially housed with makeshift shelters of straw bales or are moved to empty barns during the lambing

Sheep wintering in 'makeshift' house

season. This shelter makes the shepherd's work more efficient and protects small lambs from cold weather, foxes and crows. Temporary shelters have the advantage of having to be dismantled each year which means that the problem of diseases being carried in buildings from one year to the next is eliminated.

Farms without permanent housing for sheep must have some arrangement to confine the sheep when they are handled during worming, culling, shearing, feet trimming, dipping and so on. Handling is achieved with a group of pens with connecting gates; the pen walls are 1.5 metres high, which is too much for sheep to jump. Many handling pens also have a sheep dip which is a concrete-lined basin to hold pesticide (usually BHC), which is deep enough to completely immerse the animal in. There are many different designs and layouts for sheep handling pens; the plant of a pen illustrated is in the Lake District near Keswick and is used to handle a large flock of Swaledales, usually kept on the fells:

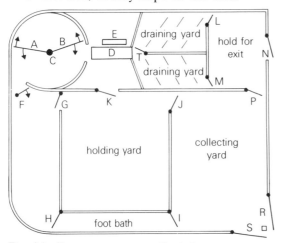

Double lines represent walls 1.5 metres high.
A and B are gates pivoted on post C which can be fixed in any position.
D is a sheep dip; see vertical section opposite.
E is a well, one metre deep, in which the shepherd stands whilst dipping.
T is a gate hinged to allow either draining yard to be filled with sheep. The pesticide drains from the sheep in these yards and runs back into the sheep dip.
The footbath is a shallow trough with a corrugated bottom.

F, G, H, J, K, L, M, N, I, P, R, and S are gates.

The circular pen can be gradually reduced in size by moving gates A and B with sheep trapped between, thus the operator who is dropping sheep into the dip does not have to run around trying to catch the next one.

Sheep in the collecting yard can be dipped either with or without a footbath, which is filled with a strong agent to kill the bacteria responsible for footrot. The footbath is similar to those at many swimming pools except the bottom is corrugated to spread the toes and allow pesticide in between. The purpose of the holding yard is to allow two flocks to be treated at the same time without mixing them up.

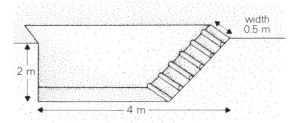

Vertical section through a sheep dip (top)
Sheep's view of an empty dip (below)

The liquid in a sheep dip is expensive and each sheep carries a lot away with it as it leaves; the draining yards allow the liquid to drain back into the dip as it drips from the animal.

Gate T allows one draining yard to be filled at a time; sheep are draining in one yard whilst the other is being filled. When the second yard is filled, the sheep (now drained) in the first one are released to the hold for exit yard. Gate T can also be used to separate sheep from lambs as they are dipped.

Water can be a problem with housed sheep as they will only drink water that is clean, fresh and *cold*. Sheep will die of thirst before they will drink dirty tepid water.

Foods and feeding

A ewe is kept for a whole year to produce a fleece and either one or two lambs for sale. With this low yield, lamb production would be uneconomic if the ewe had to be given a lot of food in addition to her grazing. There are however certain times of the year where additional feeding is economic; these are:

1. In October before the ewes are mated, as extra food stimulates ovulation and increases the likelihood of twins. This feeding is known as *flushing*. Flushing also has the effect of shortening the lambing season, as ewes in good condition are more likely to become pregnant the first time they mate.

If a ewe fails to become pregnant, how long will it be before she is next in breeding condition?
...Q.4

2. In deep winter when grazing becomes too poor to keep the flock in fair condition extra feeding may be required. Moderate falls of snow do not prevent sheep from grazing as they use their front feet to uncover the grass.
3. A month or so before the lambs are due to arrive. During the four weeks before birth the unborn lamb more than doubles in weight; the ewe needs extra food at this time to supply the unborn lamb and to build her body reserves for the forthcoming lactation. Additional feeding in late stages of pregnancy is known as *steaming up* and this is a common practice with dairy cattle.
4. During the first few weeks of lactation. This period is often just before the growth of spring grass and, at this time, lambs obtain nearly all their requirements from their dams, although they begin to graze a little when they are only a few days old.
5. Creep feeding of lambs. Some shepherds give their lambs concentrates when they are very young; this helps them to grow quickly and to make good use of spring grass when it becomes available.

What is a creep? ...Q.5

6. Fattening early lambs. The first lambs to market command a high price; extra food speeds their growth and gets them there a little earlier.

The extra foods mentioned above can take the form of additional grazing, root crops, kale, rape, rolled barley or compounded food in the form of nuts or pellets; rootcrops, kale and rape are grazed as growing crops. Where concentrates are used amounts in excess of 0.5 kg per animal per day are uneconomic. Bulky foods must be given in larger amounts.

Minerals are often in short supply, especially on poor mountain and moorland grazings, and these are made good by supplying large blocks of salt, to which other minerals have been added.

A mineral block inside a concrete container

Mineral blocks are placed in the fields for the sheep to lick at will. One method of giving lambs good pasture is known as forward creep grazing:

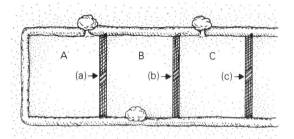

The grazing area is divided into a number of paddocks and each paddock grazed in turn. By means of a creep the lambs have access to each new paddock before the ewes.

The flock is confined to paddock A but the lambs can also enter paddock B through creep (a). After the grass in paddock A has been grazed the flock is moved into paddock B, creep (a) closed and creep (b) opened to allow the lambs into paddock C and so on.

Forward creep grazing has the additional advantage in that lambs are less likely to become hosts to internal parasites dropped in the pasture by the adults.

Task 6.3

Read the passage below and answer the questions which follow.

A Year in my Life – written by a shepherd

'My first job when I return from my holidays at the end of September is to select the breeding flock from the old ewes and the eighteen month old ewe lambs. Sandy, my dog, collects the old ewes and I watch them run. I will remove those that appear lame and any with lack-lustre wool when I go through them individually. When the ewes are safely in a pen I handle each in turn.

'First I pick the ewe up to feel her weight; any that feel light are transferred to the 'cull' pen. If the ewe is in good condition I look into her mouth and examine the incisor teeth; eight good incisors in the bottom jaw (there are none in the top jaw) are necessary if the ewe is to harvest enough grass to feed herself and her lambs. If the mouth is OK I sit the ewe on her tail and examine her udder; she must have two sound glands and teats. Any ewe that passes all these tests is released into the field as part of the breeding flock.

'I make up the number of the breeding flock to 400 by selecting the best of the eighteen month old ewe lambs; the unwanted ewe-lambs are sold through the market to other farmers and the cull ewes are sold for slaughter.

'Once selected the new breeding flock is flushed on fresh pasture and two hectares of rape grown especially for the purpose. Well-flushed ewes have lots of twins and a short lambing season. Three weeks later I fit each of the eight rams with a harness which holds a raddle pad between his front legs; this pad will mark the back of each ewe as she mates and I can keep a check on lambing dates and repeat services. As I rear my own replacement ewes I have to buy new rams every two years or there would be interbreeding, with rams serving their own daughters.

'A sheep's oestrous cycle is about 17 days, so all the ewes should mate during the first three weeks. Some will not and others may not hold to the first service, so I leave the rams in for six weeks altogether before removing them. Many shepherds run the rams with the ewes throughout the winter. I don't like doing this as I find the odd lambs that are born late to be more trouble than they are worth.

'During the first half of pregnancy I keep the flock on rather poor pasture as they must not become fat during this period. In February, Sandy and I bring the flock nearer home to better pastures and a little hay to improve their diet. Underfed ewes produce weak lambs, which often die.

'During March I steam them up with a few sheep nuts, up to half a kilo a day for each ewe depending upon the quality of the grazing. At this time I reduce the amount of hay as there will be less room for the lambs to develop if the gut is

A flock of Blackface sheep in the Scottish Highlands

filled with roughage. Half way through March, when lambing is about to begin, I move the flock into the field by my house where I can keep an eye on them and tend them in the night if necessary. There is also a good shed in this field for the ewe and her new born lambs during those first few vital days of life.

'Most ewes lamb on their own but some require help from me. I wash my hands, soap them well and carefully insert one hand into the vagina of the distressed ewe. I find the front feet and head of the lamb and gently ease it out as the ewe pushes with the muscles of her uterus.

'As soon as the lamb is born the mother licks it all over; this stimulates the lamb which is soon up on its wobbly legs seeking its first feed of colostrum. If any of the ewes have triplets I take one away and give it to a mother who has lost her lamb. This used to be a difficult job, involving skinning a dead lamb and transferring the coat to the foster lamb to persuade the ewe to accept it.

'I now have a "lamb adopter" which holds the ewe whilst the lamb suckles, after a day or so mother and lamb accept each other and can be released. Before I release lambs to the field I dock them by fitting a rubber ring high up the tail; the part of the tail below the ring receives no blood and drops off within a few weeks. Undocked tails become dirty and make ideal sites for blowfly attack, and a flock without tails suffer much less from this pest. Many mountain flocks are left undocked as they need tails to keep their hindparts warm in severe weather.

'I used to castrate all male lambs at this time by fitting a rubber ring on the scrotum above the testicles. Castrated lambs are easier to manage as they get older, also the meat of a castrated animals is slightly better.

'This year I am trying a bunch of lambs without castrating them as the vet tells me that entire animals grow more quickly, have leaner meat and a better food conversion rate than castrated ones.

'I always enjoy the month of May and watch the ewes and lambs thrive on early summer grass. My flock has little trouble with internal parasites and liver fluke seems to be a thing of the past since the introduction of systemic pesticides. Forward creep grazing is my way of bringing the lambs on early and controlling worms, but I do dose the flock once at the end of May as a precaution.

'As the weather gets warmer the yolk rises in the fleece and the adults can be sheared. In this part of the country this happens by about the second week of June. Sandy and I gather about sixty ewes each morning. I use electric shears which look rather like large hair clippers. I catch a sheep, sit it on its tail and hold its head between my legs. In this position I clip the fleece from the underparts working from between the front legs downwards. I twist the animal on to its side whilst I clip the back and the fleece comes off in one piece. My daughter assists by rolling up each fleece and bagging them ready for the Wool Marketing Board to collect.

'Two or three weeks after shearing the sheep have grown enough wool to hold some dip and all the sheep, including the lambs, are dipped. Dipping is a two-man job and my neighbour and I share this – we dip my sheep one day and his the next. The village policeman checks to make sure the law is being complied with and each sheep spends two minutes in the dip and is completely submerged for part of the time.

'Soon after dipping, when the lambs are about four months old I wean them, taking the ewes to poor pasture while their milk dries up. The lambs continue on good pasture and quickly fatten. Once they reach 40 kilos liveweight they go to market and are purchased by butchers. By the beginning of September all the lambs are sold and I go for a holiday.'

Which ewes does the shepherd reject when selecting the breeding flock?

Why are ewes kept on poor pasture during the first part of pregancy?

For what reason do lowland sheep have their tails docked?

How many ewes per ram does the shepherd allow?

What is a ewe's first action after her lamb is born?

The sheepdog

The shepherd's work would be virtually impossible without a good working dog. Popular breeds 'of old' like the old English sheepdog have been replaced the world over by the border collie. Every shepherd had at least one of these intelligent, hardworking animals, man and dog working as a team. Collie puppies often show an inbred urge to herd and spend hours in the farmyard gathering hens or ducks into a corner and keeping them there.

Once a puppy has confidence in the shepherd, usually by the age of four months, he is introduced to sheep. At this time he is kept on a lead to get used to the sight and smell of the larger animals; he is not allowed to run until he is strong enough to outpace the sheep or he will develop the habit of barking after them.

When accustomed to sheep the pup is trained with a few old ones which are used to being worked by a dog. Although an older dog is often to hand one dog is not used to train another; the older dog resents the young one and the pup wants to play with the older dog instead of working the sheep.

During its training the sheepdog learns to think for himself and work with very few commands; command may be by voice or whistle, depending upon the wishes of the shepherd, but the same sound always means the same thing. The better shepherds train their dogs by encouragement and rewards for the correct movements and not by punishments for incorrect ones.

The sheepdog's natural habit is to gather sheep and bring them to the shepherd; considerable skill and patience are required to teach the dog to do the opposite and drive the sheep along with his master.

The final stage of training is to teach a dog to 'shed', that is to separate one sheep from the flock; some dogs are not able to hold a single sheep but can be taught to hold a small group which contains the wanted animal.

Working dogs usually have the run of the shepherd's house and are well fed with cooked meat and whole cereals (brown bread, never white) and milk. The sheepdog is treated regularly for internal parasites and vaccinated against distemper and other common diseases. It is important that pet dogs in the same household receive similar medication.

Biology of the sheep

A healthy sheep at rest has: a respiration rate of 12–20 per minute; a pulse rate of 70–80 per minute; and a temperature of 40°C.

The gestation period of the sheep is five calendar months (150 days). Oestrus occurs only during the last four months of the year (the actual time depends upon the breed and the district) and the heat period lasts for one day and recurs every 17 days unless the ewe is pregnant. The Dorset Horn will take the ram in May and will breed twice a year.

Reproduction, circulation and respiration of sheep are similar to that of the pig. Refer to *GCSE Rural Science 1* to revise these.

Dentition and milk secretion are similar to that of the ox and are described in Chapter 7 on pages 134 and 135.

Feeding and digestion

The incisor teeth of the sheep protrude and the top lip is split. This enables the animal to bite off selected herbage much closer to the ground than cattle are able to.

The food is swallowed without chewing and passes down the oesophagus into the rumen where it remains until cudding starts. If the sheep is left undisturbed for half an hour after feeding ceases, the contents of the rumen are brought back into the mouth, a bolus at a time. The bolus is masticated, swallowed and replaced by another; this process is continued for periods of up to two hours at a time. Animals which chew the cud are called *ruminants*.

Name two other farm animals which are ruminants. ...Q.6

The digestive system

The digestive system of the ruminant is designed to digest large quantities of plants, mostly grasses, which are too hard for simple-stomached animals like pig and man to digest:

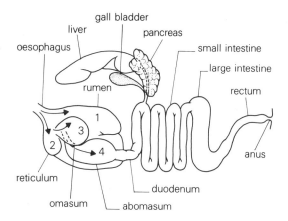

Task 6.4

Observe a number of sheep (or cattle) taking care not to disturb them. Select one animal and keep it under continuous observation for half an hour. Using a stopwatch record its activities each minute on a chart you have previously prepared.

Tick the appropriate box each minute and when complete transfer the information to a histogram or pie diagram.

During this task observe the animal carefully. If grazing, watch how the herbage is selected; try to time the number of bites per minute. Or, in cudding, how long each cud is chewed and what is the timelag between swallowing one cud and the arrival of the next.

Minutes	1	2	3	4	5	6	7	8 ...	30
Grazing									
Cudding									
Nursing									
Suckling									
Standing									
Urinating									
Defecating									
Grooming									
Feeding									

The end of the oesophagus forms three compartments which connect to the stomach. Although it is not strictly true, the ruminant is often said to have four stomachs.

The four 'stomachs' of a lamb

The first compartment (1) is called the *rumen* and is large, filling most of the abdominal cavity. Inside the rumen live thousands of millions of bacteria and protozoa (one-celled animals). The bacteria feed upon the grass, particularly the hard part (the cellulose) which most animals are unable to digest. The action of bacteria upon cellulose produces chemicals called 'fatty acids' which pass through the wall of the rumen into the sheep's bloodstream and provide energy for the sheep.

```
                eaten by
                bacteria                  absorbed by
Cellulose ─────────────→ Fatty acids ───→ sheep to
                      ╲                   provide energy
                       ╲→ More bacteria
```

The bacteria which multiply rapidly in the warm, moist conditions inside the sheep are eaten by the protozoa which also multiply rapidly. Millions of protozoa and bacteria pass from the rumen and travel along the sheep's gut where they are digested.

What is important is that the plant protein in the grass is converted to animal protein by the organisms inside the rumen and this is used by the sheep to build muscle.

Plant protein ── converted by bacteria ──→ Animal protein

The organisms inside the sheep get warmth, moisture, protection and food provided by the sheep. The sheep has a supply of fatty acids and animal protein from the organisms. Sheep and organisms obtain benefit from living together; this is an example of *symbiosis*.

The activity of the micro-organisms inside the rumen produces a large quantity of gas which the sheep gets rid of by burping.

The second compartment (2) is called the *reticulum*. This is lined with many pockets, some of which are hexagonal. This lining prevents unmasticated food from leaving the rumen and helps to make the boluses which form the cud. The reticulum is also a fluid reservoir which supplies fluid to the other compartments when required.

The third compartment (3) is called the *omasum*. This is lined with tissue that resembles the pages of a book. The surfaces of the pages are very rough. As food passes through the omasum the pages rasp together grinding it even smaller.

The fourth compartment (4) is called the *abomasum* and is the true stomach. Unlike the other three compartments, the abomasum is lined with glands which produce gastric juice.

The *liver* produces a fluid called bile which flows along a duct into the gut and aids digestion. The liver also acts as a food store. The *pancreas* produces enzymes which assist the bile in digestion.

The *small intestine* provides the surface area through which the products of digestion enter the bloodstream.

Where else in the sheep's alimentary canal does absorption take place? ...Q.7

The *large intestine* removes excess water from the contents of the gut. The *rectum* stores faeces until they are passed through the anus.

Pests and diseases of sheep

There are over sixty disorders of sheep caused by bacteria, viruses, internal and external parasites, deficiencies and poisoning.

Name a virus disease that affects sheep....Q.8

Pulpy kidney

This is caused by a bacterium (*Clostridium welchii*) which lives in the bowel. The bacterium produces toxins (poisons) which rapidly destroy the kidneys of young lambs, and other organs in older sheep. Symptoms: apparently healthy lambs from 3 to 18 weeks old suddenly die; postmortem examination reveals the kidney has degenerated and has a 'pulpy' appearance.

Prevention
A sudden change of diet from a low plane of nutrition to a high one creates conditions in the bowel for the rapid multiplication of the bacteria and any changes in the diet should be made gradually.

Ewes can be vaccinated in the autumn, and the vaccine causes the blood of the sheep to produce antibodies which destroy these particular bacteria. The lambs obtain enough of the antibodies from their dams' colostrum to protect them for the first ten weeks of life.

Footrot

Caused by a bacterium (*Fusiformis nodosus*) which invades the soft tissue of the feet. This causes a progressive lameness; first the animal limps a little, gradually the foot becomes too painful to put on the floor and the animal walks on three legs and kneels to graze. Usually a number of animals become infected at the same time. On examination the foot is found to be painful to pressure and there is a foul smelling discharge.

Treatment
This is done by careful trimming of the feet to remove excess horn and dipping in disinfectant. The treatment is repeated until no further footrot is seen. Once the flock is free from this disease it will remain so unless it is brought into contact with infected sheep or allowed onto infected pasture.

Prevention
Sheep should be kept from wet pastures wherever possible as such ground favours this disease. The organism cannot live on the soil for more than two weeks so pastures which have carried infected animals should be rested for this period before re-introducing sheep.

Sheep scab

This is a notifiable disease caused by a parasitic mite (*Psotoptes conmunes*):

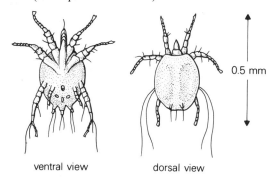

ventral view   dorsal view

Enforcement of dipping regulations eradicated sheep scab from the UK by 1952. Following relaxation of the regulations and the spraying of sheep instead of dipping them, it reappeared in 1973.

Symptoms
There are no symptoms during the summer as the mite remains dormant in folds of skin during this period. In winter the mites become active and their hosts suffer intense irritation and spend much time rubbing against posts or nibbling the areas they can reach with their teeth. Scabs form on the body and wool falls away.

The mite is just visible to the naked eye and spends its entire life on the sheep. Six of the eight legs carry suckers that give a firm hold on the skin whilst the sharp mouth parts pierce the skin and feed on the cell sap.

Sheep suffering from scab

After mating the females lay eggs around the edge of the scabs in groups of five; during a five week life each female will lay some 100 eggs. Each egg hatches two days later into a six-legged larva which feeds for four days before becoming adult. The females outnumber the males by about four to one; mating takes place after the final moult and egg laying begins. The life cycle is completed in fourteen days.

Control

The mite is killed and the disease cured by dipping the infected sheep in a dip containing gamma HCH or other chemical approved by the Ministry of Agriculture.

Strike

Strike is very common in the UK. It is caused by a fly – the greenbottle (*Lucilia sericata*) – which lays its eggs on dirty areas of fleece. The eggs hatch into larvae which feed on the skin and flesh of the living sheep – the larvae being similar in appearance to the maggots fishermen use.

Life cycle

Eggs, almost 2 mm long and pale yellow, are laid at the base of the wool against the skin. The eggs hatch after an incubation period which varies between ten hours and three days. The head, which is at the pointed end of the larva, has a mouth with two hooks to pierce the skin upon which the larva first feeds. The larva enters the flesh and feeds rapidly for about three days. When fully grown (about 12 mm long) the larva emerges from the flesh, falls to the ground, burrows into the soil and pupates.

During the three week pupation period the pupa changes from a light colour to a very dark brown. The metallic green flies which emerge live for a month and are capable of flights of up to ten miles. This species over winters as mature larvae which hibernate in the soil before pupating.

Symptoms

Sheep infected with strike stamp their legs and wag their tails rapidly; they often leave the flock and stand in a dejected manner with drooping heads and arched backs. The wool in the area of the strike wound becomes wet and matted and, if pulled, comes away revealing an inflamed wound, which smells badly and in which burrowing larvae can be found. The sheep quickly loses condition and if the infection is extensive dies within a few days.

Control

All larvae should be removed at the time of treatment and destroyed. If a sheep dies of strike the carcase should be burned or treated with a strong disinfectant and burial should be as deep as possible. Dirty wool, particularly around the tail region, should be cut off, also wool from the inside of the thighs. Shepherds call this treatment 'dagging' and 'crutching'.

Dipping sheep in a gamma-BHC dip is effective against strike as this chemical persists in the fleece for two or more weeks after dipping.

Liver fluke *(Fasciola hepatica)*

Until recently this internal parasite was responsible for large losses in both cattle and sheep, especially in the areas of high rainfall. Meat inspectors were rejecting up to one third of all cattle and sheep livers because they contained flukes; however with the introduction of systemic pesticides this parasite is becoming quite rare.

Description

The adult fluke is a flat, leaflike worm about 25 mm long which lives in the livers of host animals. Cattle, sheep, rabbits and, sometimes, man can harbour flukes.

Damage

In sheep, damage by liver fluke has two forms:

Acute form in which animals that appear healthy die suddenly. Post mortem examination of these animals reveals a ruptured liver and much blood stained fluid in the intestines. The

The adult liver fluke

25 mm

actue form is caused by large numbers of immature migrating larvae.

Chronic form in which the animal gradually loses condition and lags behind the rest of the flock. A soft watery swelling develops under the jaws and the animal's belly swells beneath the fleshless bones. Post mortem examination shows the liver to be hard with thickened ducts (pipes) and containing many adult flukes.

Life cycle

Adult flukes in the liver lay eggs which pass into the intestines with the bile. The eggs pass out of the animal with the faeces. In warm moist conditions the eggs hatch into larvae which swim for a few hours and die. If, during this swimming period, a larva encounters a mud snail it burrows into it and migrates to the liver. Inside the liver of the snail, the larva multiplies into thousands of tadpole-like larvae which leave the snail and swim up blades of grass. Each larva loses its tail, becomes a tough cyst attached to the grass and remains dormant for several months.

If a grazing animal (cow, sheep or rabbit) consumes the cyst along with the grass, the cyst breaks open in the duodenum and the young fluke inside burrows into the blood stream and is pumped around the body. On reaching the liver the fluke leaves the blood stream and burrows into the organ, feeding on blood and tissue. About six weeks later it is fully grown and producing large numbers of eggs.

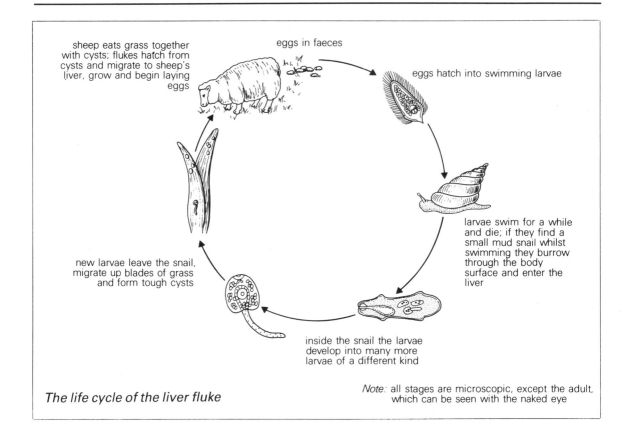

The life cycle of the liver fluke

Note: all stages are microscopic, except the adult, which can be seen with the naked eye

Control

The mud snail is a very small mollusc about 8 mm in length which lives in wet places, particularly around watering points in the foot prints of animals. Without the mud snail the liver fluke cannot complete its life cycle. Good control can be obtained on many farms by reducing snail numbers by land drainage and spraying wet areas with copper sulphate or other snail killers. Where drainage is not possible wet areas can be fenced off to keep the animals from them. Unfortunately fluke will persist in these areas if rabbits are present.

All stages of the liver fluke present in the host animal can be killed by administering modern drugs (*diamphenethide* and *hexachloroethane*) by mouth, according to manufacturers' instructions. Multi-dose applicators are available which enable whole flocks to be treated quickly.

Questions: Sheep

1. Write single sentences to answer the following questions:
   (a) What does the word *crimp* mean when applied to the wool of sheep?
   (b) Why is the bottom of a sheeps' foot-bath corrugated?
   (c) What is the advantage of *flushing* ewes?
   (d) Barley fed to sheep is not fed whole but rolled flat – why is this?
   (e) How does forward creep grazing help to control internal parasites in lambs?
   (f) Why do some shepherds leave the tup with the ewes for only six weeks?
   (g) Upon what does the bacteria in a sheep's rumen feed?
   (h) What effect has the introduction of systemic pesticides had upon liver flukes?
   (i) How long can the bacteria *Fusiformis nodosus* survive in pasture?

2.

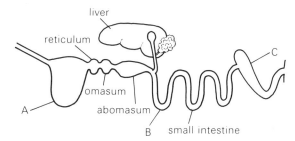

Digestive system of a sheep

   (a) Name the parts A, B and C.
   (b) What is a cud? How does cudding aid digestion?
   (c) Describe how you would rear an orphan lamb from birth to weaning.

3. The law states that sheep have to be dipped at certain times.
   (a) Describe with words and diagrams how a sheep is dipped.
   (b) What is the purpose of dipping sheep?
   (c) The draining area where sheep stand after dipping drains back into the dip; suggest *two* reasons for this.
   (d) In what way can sheep dipping cause environmental damage?

4. Describe the life cycle of an internal parasite of sheep and show how knowledge of this life cycle has led to a number of different ways of controlling this organism in a flock of sheep.

5.

Month	Management tasks
September	
October	

   (a) Make a chart like the one above showing all the months of the year.
   (b) Complete the empty boxes showing the tasks a shepherd responsible for a flock of breeding ewes has to do.

6. (a) Describe a system of controlled grazing, suitable for ewes with lambs, which gives the lambs access to fresh grass before the ewes.
   (b) Describe all the advantages a shepherd expects to obtain from the system you have described.

7 Cattle

The word 'cattle' refers to oxen belonging to the genus *Bos*. This genus includes buffalo, bison, yak, the humped cattle of Africa and Asia, as well as the European domestic cattle. With the exception of buffalo, all the animals in this list will interbreed although the progeny (offspring) of some crosses may be infertile.

Archaeological evidence from Babylon indicates that cattle have been domesticated for over 5000 years. In Europe, domestic cattle were widespread in the New Stone Age (Neolithic period) and genuine wild cattle roamed the plains until the last one was killed in Poland in 1627.

Before the time of Christ, British native cattle were small, brown and had short horns, characteristics which survive today in the Jersey and Kerry breeds. The Romans introduced large white cattle, the descendants of which can be seen at Chartley and other large houses where park cattle are kept. The Anglo-Saxons brought with them red cattle from which our Devon breed descended. Norse invaders brought the polls (no horns) and in the seventeenth century the ancestors of the Ayrshire and Shorthorn breeds were imported from the Netherlands. Two hundred years later many black and white cattle were imported from the same country to be kept in towns for milk production. From these animals the United Kingdom's most numerous breed has developed – the British Friesian. No new breeds were imported from 1880 until 1961 when 26 Charolais bulls arrived from France and, because of the large muscles on the hindquarters and low proportion of fat, quickly found favour with British butchers. Since that time, twelve other breeds have been imported from the continent, increasing the number of breeds in this country to over 30.

Cattle products

Cattle are kept to convert grass, grain and other crops into protein-rich foods for man.

1. Beef

Beef is the flesh of the ox; the average annual consumption in the UK is just over 28 kg per person. This amounts to one million tonnes, three quarters of which is home-produced. The killing out percentage of good beef cattle is 60.

What weight will the butcher receive from the slaughter of a bullock that weighed 500 kg on the hoof? ...Q.1

The texture and fat content of beef vary according to the part of the animal from which it was cut. The different parts (cuts) have different names.

The best beef is marbled. That is, it has small deposits of fat throughout the muscle (red meat). Poor quality beef from breeds like the Jersey has the fat deposited as a separate layer over the muscle. In addition to the joints shown in the diagram the animal provides liver, heart, kidney, ox-tail, tripe, suet and tongue. The hides of slaughtered cattle are the main source of leather.

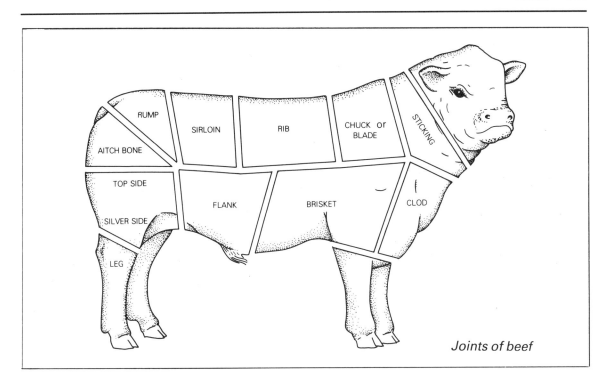

Joints of beef

2. Milk

Liquid milk consumption in the UK is over 0.4 litres a person a day and is an important part of the diet, providing protein, sugar, fats, minerals and vitamins.

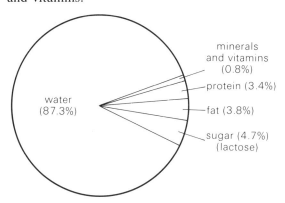

The composition of milk

It is illegal to sell milk with less than 3% butterfat or less than 8.5% other solids (s.n.f., solids not fat, i.e. all solid matter other than butterfat contained in milk). Such milk has probably been diluted either by adding water or removing cream.

Task 7.1

1. Take two pints of fresh milk, stand one upside down and the other upright and leave overnight.
2. Measure the depth of cream on each bottle. Describe and try to explain the difference.
3. Use a pipette to obtain 20 ml of milk from near to the bottom of the upright bottle, and transfer it to a clean test-tube.
4. Draw off 20 ml of cream in the same way and transfer to another test-tube.
5. Take two test-tubes – one in each hand. Cover with the thumbs and shake vigorously.
6. Continue shaking and observe every minute or so.
7. In one tube a lump of butter forms, the other remains unchanged. Note the liquid in which the butter is floating. This is buttermilk.
8. Pour away the buttermilk and wash the butter in cold water.
9. Taste the butter.
10. Mix a little table salt with the remaining butter and taste again.

One litre of milk makes 40 g of butter (this varies according to breed of cow, age and feeding). In practice, butter is made from cream that has been separated from the milk. The remaining milk (skim milk) is reduced to powder for use in the food industry or for inclusion in animal feeding stuff.

Cheese

Butter and cheese making is carried on in large urban factories and is no longer regarded as a significant part of the rural economy. Cheese is made from whole milk. One litre of milk makes about 100 g of cheese, leaving whey, a liquid by-product, which is fed to pigs or used in the manufacture of margarine:

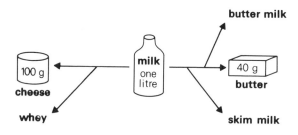

Minerals in milk

Minerals are present in milk in the following proportions:
Potassium 28%; Phosphorus 27%; Calcium 20%; Sodium 8%; Magnesium 3%; Iron 1%; Others 1%; Chlorine 12%.

Task 7.2

Using the figures quoted, draw a histogram to show the proportions of different minerals present in cow's milk.

Breeds of cattle

The breeds of cattle can be divided into three groups: beef breeds, dairy breeds, and dual purpose breeds.

Dairy breeds

Ayrshire; British Friesian; Guernsey; Jersey; Holstein.

Beef breeds

Beef Shorthorn; Welsh Black; Hereford; Aberdeen Angus; Devon; South Devon; Sussex; Highland; Galloway; Lincoln Red; Charolais; Simmenthal; Blonde d'Aquitaine; Chianina; Limousin; Luing; Marchingiana; Maine-Anjou; MIR; Murray Grey; Ramagnola.

Dual purpose breeds

Red Poll; Brown Swiss; Gelbvich; Dexter; Dairy Shorthorn.

Milk production is now very intensive and specialised and over 99 per cent of all dairy herds consist of pure dairy breeds.

Differences between beef and dairy cattle

Dairy cattle have much finer bones than beef cattle. Their body is wedge shaped with the thin edge at the shoulders and the thick edge at the hind quarters. Dairy cattle have large udders with a thick milk vein protruding for about 30 cm forward of the udder.

Beef cattle are like a long oxo cube on four legs. They are not wedge shaped, their underbelly line is parallel with the line along their back and the top of their shoulders is broad and flat. The hind quarters on either side of the tail are rounded with double muscles rather like a horse. Thick muscles cover the shoulder blades and, unlike the dairy breeds, the hip bones do not protrude.

Task 7.3

Read the account above and look at the photographs in this chapter (or better still examine actual cattle). Make a large copy of the chart on page 117 and complete it with as much detail as possible.

Cattle

Beef – Limousin

Dairy – Friesian

	Dairy type	Beef type
Body shape		
Muscles		
Udder		
Shoulders		

The main difference between dairy and beef breeds is the way in which their bodies use food. The body chemistry of beef cattle converts surplus food to flesh and the body chemistry of dairy cows converts surplus food into milk.

Cross breeds

A dairy cow will have four or five calves during her working life. Only one of these calves will be needed to replace her; the remainder can be grown into beef. A lot of beef is thus bred from the dairy herd. To improve the suitability of these animals for beef production, dairy farmers cross their average and below average yielders with a beef bull.

Why do dairy farmers not use a beef bull on their highest yielders? ...Q.2

With the exception of British Friesians, pure dairy cattle are of little use for beef. Bull calves of these breeds not wanted for breeding are slaughtered when a few days old.

The British Friesian

Over half the 14 million cattle in Britain are British Friesians.

Originating in the Dutch province of Friesland, the animals are black and white, in clear distinct patches; they have four white socks and a white hair switch to the tail. Weighing 650 kg, the Friesian is the heaviest dairy breed; it also gives the highest yields of milk.

Due to a recessive gene some Friesians are red and white.

Ayrshire

Bred from native and Dutch cattle, this breed has been widely exported and there are large numbers in the USA, Canada, Finland, South Africa the New Zealand. The colour is red and white and cows weigh about 550 kg; they perform well in hilly areas considered to be unsuitable for Friesians. Milk yields are less than Friesians' but the milk is slightly better in quality, containing almost 4% fat in small droplets, which makes it ideal for baby feeding and cheese making.

Jersey

This breed originated in the island of Jersey where all cattle imports have been banned since 1763. The small fine-boned cattle weigh up to 350 kg; the colour varies from almost black, through various shades of fawn to almost white; there is a ring of lighter colour round the muzzle. Milk yields are high compared with body weight and the fat content exceeds 5%, giving a deep cream line and a yellow colour. Jersey and Guernsey milk (gold top) commands a higher price than that of other breeds. Jersey cattle mature quickly; heifers (young females) calve at just over two years old.

An Ayrshire cow

Hereford

A pure beef breed from the county of Hereford, it is red in colour with a white face, underbelly, and switch. The white face is a dominant characteristic shown by all pure-bred and cross-bred calves. Dairy farmers often use Hereford bulls, so market buyers can tell by the white face that the calf was sired by a Hereford bull. Herefords fatten readily on grass and are widely used in the USA as ranch cattle.

A Jersey cow

Welsh Black

A hardy beef breed with good milking qualities, making it most suitable for suckling calves at pasture.

Aberdeen Angus

Black, hornless, cattle bred in the north-east of Scotland. The breed is the almost perfect beef animal, quickly growing into a solid block of high quality meat. Their very small heads make calving easy and, for this reason, many dairy farmers use Aberdeen Angus bulls on their dairy

A Hereford bull

heifers. In addition the black colour and hornless characteristics are dominant and all calves are black and polled irrespective of the breed of dairy cow.

Charolais

Originating in France, the Charolais is now widely used to produce beef from the dairy herd. It is a large animal which grows rapidly and its flesh has little fat. The heavy muscles on the hind-quarters are a result of being bred as a draught animal, i.e. for pulling the plough, or a cart.

Welsh Black bull

Aberdeen Angus bull

Charolais cow with her calf

Task 7.4

Study the Milk Marketing Board figures for inseminations during a recent year and show the relative popularity of:
(a) the various dairy breeds in a pie diagram.
    (Friesian = 341°   Ayrshire = 4.5°
     Guernsey = 5.5°   Jersey   = 9°)
(b) the various beef breeds in a histogram.

Dairy breeds:
Ayrshire	13 500
Friesian (including Canadian Holstein)	1 032 000
Guernsey	16 500
Jersey	26 000

Beef breeds:
Aberdeen Angus	53 000
Charolais	155 000
South Devon	4000
Hereford	336 000
Limousin	194 000
Murrey Grey	6000
Simmental	39 000
Welsh Black	3000
Others	25 000

Rare breeds

Some breeds of cattle are in danger of extinction. The Milk Marketing Board inseminated over three million cattle during a recent year, of which only 30 were Longhorns, 10 were Shetland, and none at all were Kerry. If breeds are lost, some characteristics (genes) will also be lost for ever. Future breeders may require some of these characteristics and the Rare Breeds Trust is attempting to save breeds from extinction for this purpose. The total of genes in all cattle breeds is called the gene 'pool' and it is important that this pool is as large as possible.

Artificial insemination (AI)

Artificial insemination means taking sperms from the male animal and introducing them, manually, to the female's uterus, thus making her pregnant without the act of mating.

In the UK a large proportion of all calvings are the result of the national AI service, introduced in 1942 by the Milk Marketing Board.

When the cow is in oestrus (breeding condition) the farmer informs the local AI centre and, within a few hours, the operator arrives and inseminates the cow with semen from the chosen breed. If the insemination is successful the cow will calve nine months later. If unsuccessful the cow will return to oestrus three weeks later and will be inseminated a second time.

Collection of semen

The bull is encouraged to mate with an artificial or real animal. As he mounts, a rubber vagina is slipped over his penis and the semen collects in a tube at the end. When diluted with egg or milk a single collection is enough to inseminate 250 cows. Diluted semen not required for immediate use has glycerine added before being frozen to −73°C.

Frozen semen remains alive for many years; indeed, the semen from outstanding bulls is often in use long after the animals have died.

Inseminating a cow

The inseminator draws a little semen into sterile tube A by withdrawing plunger B:

Inserting one (scrubbed) hand into the cow's anus he feels the position of the cervix through the wall of the rectum. With the other hand he gently passes the tube through the vagina to the cervix. The semen is deposited by depressing the plunger. The whole operation takes only three or four minutes:

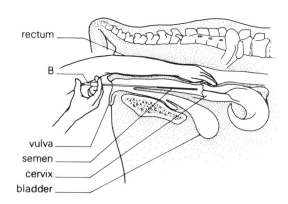

Advantages of AI

1. Only the best bulls are used for AI. These bulls will produce many thousands of offspring by AI instead of the few hundred they would have produced by natural service. This has the effect of improving the national herd.
2. A farmer has no need to keep a bull; this reduces his workload and improves farm safety.
3. Not only does AI give farmers a choice of breed; it allows them to use several different breeds. For example a dairy farmer with a Friesian herd could use Aberdeen Augus semen on his heifers, Hereford on his below average milkers, and Friesian on his best milkers.

Why use Aberdeen Angus on the heifers?
...Q.3
Why use Friesian on the best milkers? ...Q.4
Why use Hereford on the below average milkers?
...Q.5

Progeny testing

Before a bull is used extensively at an AI centre its progeny (offspring) are tested to ensure that his special qualities are inherited. A young bull is selected by visual inspection and his pedigree record.

Before the bull is one year old, collections of his semen are made and cows in different herds inseminated with it. The calves from these inseminations are compared with the progeny of other bulls by inspection, growth rate, age of maturity, yield and quality of milk, and so on – a process that takes four or more years, during which time the bull is unused.

If the progeny of the new bull compares well he will be added to the list of working bulls at an AI centre. If his progeny compare badly he will be slaughtered.

Embryo transplants

Artificial insemination provides the means of obtaining large numbers of offspring from an outstanding male. Embryo transplanting enables an outstanding female to produce a large number of offspring.

An embryo (a developing fertilised egg) is removed from the uterus of a superior cow and transplanted into the uterus of another cow, who will then bear the superior cow's calf.

The system works as follows:

1. The donor cow is given hormones to induce the release of many eggs from her ovaries instead of the usual one.
2. A few days later the cow is inseminated.
3. Seven days later the embryos are washed out of the uterus by a veterinary surgeon.
4. Each recipient cow has an incision made in her flank, and the horn of the uterus is exposed and pierced and the embryo implanted.
5. The recipient cows deliver (about nine months later) calves which are the genetic progeny of the donor cow.

Embryos frozen at −196°C will remain viable for long periods and can be transported around the world before being implanted. A container, one metre in diameter and one metre high, will hold fifty 'potential cattle' in the form of frozen embryos. This method of export has the advantages of being cheap and disease-free, as well as relieving live animals of the stress of long journeys.

Removing fertilised embryos

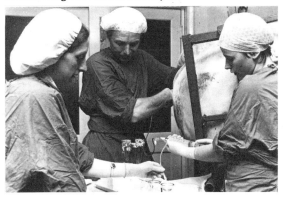

Pedigree

For more than a hundred years the breed societies have been responsible for improving the quality of the nation's cattle stock. They achieve this by setting standards and encouraging competition amongst members with shows and sales.

Animals which comply with the standards set by a society are entered on a register known as the *herdbook*. Details of ancestry and commercial performance, weight at a certain age, rate of growth, milk yield, quality of milk, and so on, are noted and animals which are entered in the herdbook are called *pedigree*.

Some herdbooks are 'closed', which means that only the progeny of pedigree animals may be entered. The Aberdeen Angus herdbook is closed and the Hereford herdbook has been closed since 1883. No new genes can be introduced into a closed book and the animals should then remain true to type.

Not all societies have closed herdbooks and it is possible for farmers with good commercial herds to grade up to full pedigree status with these societies. Grading up is a slow process, and a herd of non-pedigree Friesians could take over fifteen years to convert to full pedigree status.

Grading up a commercial Friesian herd to pedigree

1. The calves and their dams are inspected by an officer of the society before the calves are thirty days old. If suitable the calves are entered on a supplementary register known as an A register.
2. The progeny of animals on the A register are entered on a B register.
3. The progeny of animals on the B register are entered on a C register.
4. The progeny of animals on the C register are eligible for entry in the herdbook as full pedigree animals.

Each pedigree Friesian has a binomial name; the first part is the herd name (like a surname) and the second part is its specific name. When registering a calf the owner has to complete a form like the one shown, which includes the colour markings of the calf.

Task 7.5

Trace the three outlines in the drawing below, and mark in the colours of the calf in the photographs (opposite) as you would if you wished to register it with the British Friesian Society.

One of the main aims of the Friesian breeders during the last decade has been to improve the percentage fat in the breed's milk. A certificate

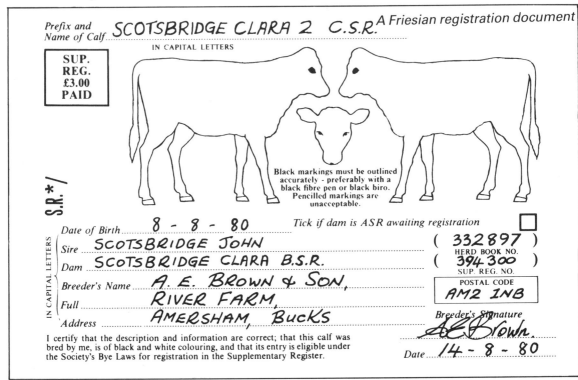

A Friesian registration document

of merit is awarded to the best animals and the letters RM (Register of Merit) are written after their names. In order to receive RM a cow must produce 8250 kg of milk in a single lactation if the butterfat content is 3.5% but only 5500 kg of milk if the butterfat content is 3.8%.

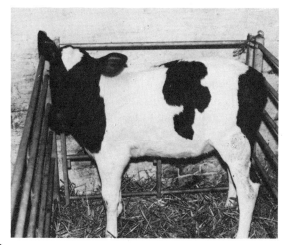

The right and left sides of the same Friesian calf

Milk recording

It is necessary for milk producers to know the yield of each cow, as feeding levels depend upon the level of production. The more milk a cow gives the more food she receives; once a week each cow's milk is weighed and recorded. Pedigree breeders have their recordings checked once a month by an independent body – National Milk Records – to prevent any malpractice.

Task 7.6

Opposite are the milk records of two animals from Mr Archer's farm, Lacta Fleur and Lacta Angela, for their second lactation.

(a) What was the total yield of each cow for this lactation?
(b) Draw a line graph with months along the horizontal axis and yield on the vertical axis. Put each cow's yield on the graph using a different coloured line for each animal.

Draw each line as a smooth curve passing through the dots and *not* as a series of straight lines joining dots. The highest point on the curve is the peak yield, and the area under the curve represents the total yield for that lactation. The cows both calved on 15 January and the recordings were all taken on the first of the month. For the purpose of the graph assume all months are of equal length.

Month	Milk yield (kg/day)	
	Lacta Fleur	*Lacta Angela*
January	0	0
February	25	40
March	30	44
April	33	40
May	37	40
June	33	34
July	32	30
August	23	28
September	21	22
October	15	22
November	10	16
December	0	0

The average percentage butterfat for both cows during this lactation was 4.02%. These animals are in the B register of the British Friesian Society.

Is Lacta Fleur a full pedigree? ...Q.6

What is the name of the herd to which the two cows belong? ...Q.7

Housing

Many breeds of cattle will live outside all winter with little or no shelter; they grow much longer coats than housed animals.

Outwintering

Outwintering animals grow more slowly than housed animals as a larger proportion of their food is used to maintain body temperature. In many areas it is soil rather than atmospheric conditions which determines whether or not the cattle are housed in winter, as cattle cannot thrive on wet muddy land. In some areas beef herds and growing dairy heifers are outwintered, receiving supplementary feeding, usually in the form of hay.

Housing for beef cattle

Many beef cattle are housed in large covered yards with fresh straw bedding added each day; the bedding builds up during the winter making a warm floor on which to lie. The atmosphere inside cattle sheds is kept as dry as possible with plenty of ventilation, care being taken to avoid floor draughts. Animals kept in yards are dehorned to allow larger numbers inside than would otherwise be possible. The yards are cleaned out once a year with a tractor and fore-loader.

Housing for dairy cattle

Many dairy cattle are housed in similar covered yards; they have to be milked twice each day and to do this a milking parlour is situated nearby together with a holding yard. Maintenance rations of silage, hay or roots are fed in the yard and each cow receives its carefully-measured ration of cake while in the milking parlour.

At milking time the animals enter the parlour a group at a time; after milking they move to a holding yard where they remain until all the herd is milked. In summer they are taken from this yard to the fields, in winter they return to the covered yard.

Why are the milked animals not allowed to return directly to the covered yard? ...Q.8

Outwintering Welsh Black cattle

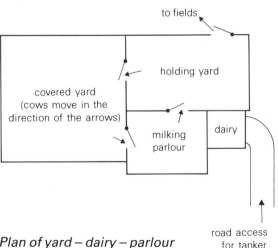

Plan of yard – dairy – parlour

Cattle

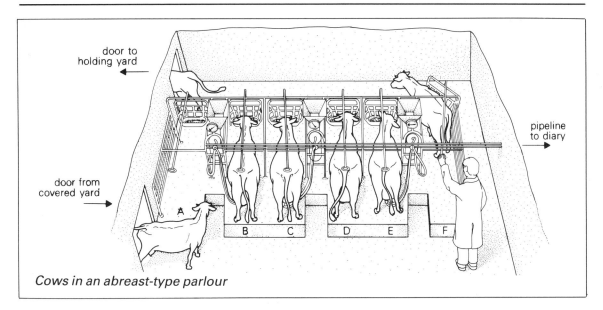

Cows in an abreast-type parlour

Milking parlours
There are many types of milking parlour, the two most common are the *abreast* and the *herringbone*..

The abreast-type parlour
In the diagram cows B, C and E are being milked. Cow D has just walked in and cows A and F are being replaced. The new cows will be prepared and then milked. The remainder of the herd enter three at a time until milking is completed. In this type of parlour one person milks about thirty cows in one hour.

Cows in a herringbone parlour

The herringbone milking parlour
In the herringbone parlour the operator works in a pit; this saves stooping as the cows' udders are at a convenient height. The working sequence:

1. The animals on one side are fed and milked, while the animals on the other side are brought in and prepared.
2. The milking machine clusters are transferred from one side to the other.
3. The milked animals are exchanged for another group.
4. The sequence is repeated until milking is complete. Up to 60 cows can be milked per hour.

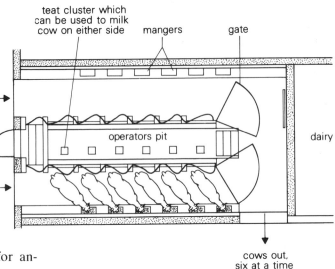

Not all dairy cows are housed in open yards; some are kept in stalls, where each animal has its own 'standing' and is secured with a yoke or chain.

Concrete or steel partitions keep the animals facing one direction.

Cows soon learn their own place and return to the same positions after grazing. Each stall is fitted with a water bowl and valve which the cow operates with her nose. The dung is removed twice daily and various automatic systems for its removal are in operation, although in many small units a shovel and wheelbarrow are used.

The milking machine clusters are carried to the cows and the milk flows along an overhead pipeline to the dairy.

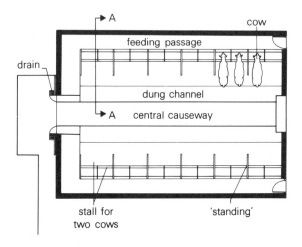
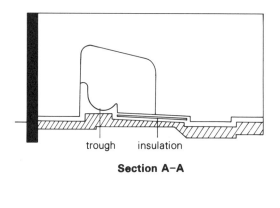

Section A–A

The milking machine

A milking machine consists of a vacuum pump, a pulsating system to alternate pressure, and a number of clusters of four-teat cups which fit over the teats. A teat cup has a rigid outer with a tight rubber lining held about 10 mm away. Vacuum holds the teat cups onto the teats and the milk flows

Cattle

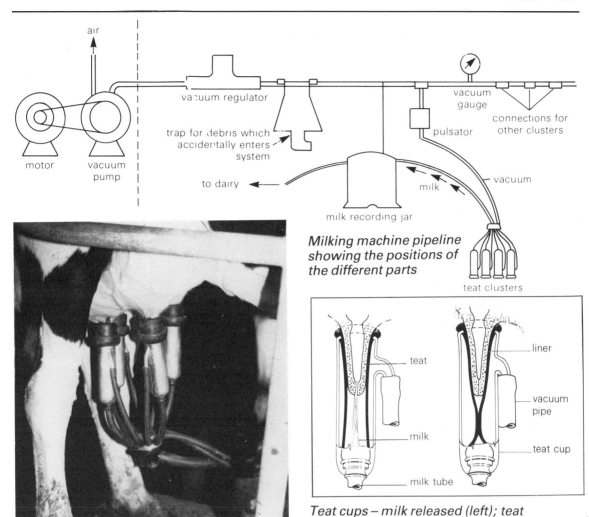

Milking machine pipeline showing the positions of the different parts

Teat cups – milk released (left); teat compressed (right)

A milking machine in use

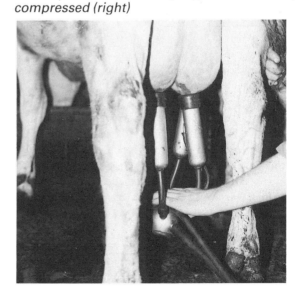

from the teats into the teat cups.

The pulsator alternates the pressure in the outer space between air pressure and vacuum. This has the effect of squeezing and relaxing the teat at regular intervals, stopping and starting the flow of milk. The action of the liner massages the teat, stimulating the blood supply and preventing damage to the tissues.

In modern parlours when milk flow stops the cluster is removed by an automatic device.

The milk flows along a single pipe from the cluster, through a filter and into a recording jar (or through a milk meter). After recording, it flows along a pipe into the dairy where it passes through a second filter before entering a large, refrigerated, stainless steel tank – the bulk tank. Milk is held in the bulk tank until collected by a road tanker which calls daily.

The tanker driver uses a dipstick to measure the volume of milk in the tank and sniffs the milk to make sure it is not tainted. After taking a sample, he connects a pipe from the bulk tank to the tanker and a pump on the vehicle quickly transfers the milk. Before leaving, the driver operates an automatic system which washes and sterilises the tank.

A milk tanker

Feeding the dairy cow

A cow needs a certain amount of food to keep her warm and healthy and to grow the calf she may be carrying. The food for these needs is called the *maintenance* ration, and usually consists of grass, silage, hay, kale or root crops. The amount of food required for maintenance depends upon the weight of the cow: the heavier the cow the more food she requires.

Which cow would require the larger maintenance ration: a Jersey or a Friesian? ...Q.9

A cow producing milk will require food additional to her maintenance ration and this extra food is called the *production* ration. If a milking cow does not have enough food she loses weight as her fat reserves are converted into milk.

Production rations are usually less bulky than maintenance rations and consist of mixtures of cereals, fishmeal, soya meal, and other foods, together with a supplement rich in minerals. These foods are referred to as *concentrates* and are usually ground and pressed into cake.

Simetimes the maintenance ration is more than enough for maintenance alone and a cow receiving it can yield milk without losing body weight.

A ration may be m + 5 which means that it is sufficient to maintain a cow and produce 5 kg of milk daily. A cow receiving m + 5 rations would

An electronic feed panel in a herringbone parlour

receive a production ration of cake for the milk she gives in excess of 5 kg.

Example:
The production ration on a farm is 2 kg of cake for each 5 kg of milk produced. If the maintenance ration is m + 5, an animal producing 10 kg would receive 2 kg of cake each day. An animal producing 25 kg would receive 8 kg of food each day.

How much cake would a cow be fed if she were producing 20 kg of milk a day? ...Q.10

Many parlours are fitted with electronic feeding devices – the control panel, shown in the photograph, allows an operator to dispense any quantity to any cow in a six-a-side herringbone parlour, by pressing the correct buttons.

In order to dispense the correct production ration the operator needs to recognise the cow, and to assist recognition, cows are numbered. Collars and tail bands of various types are in use but the most effective method is freeze branding.

Branding irons are dipped in liquid nitrogen to make them cold and placed on a black or brown part of the cow. The cold metal freezes the skin and causes a weal which soon heals, leaving a bald patch. The hair which regrows on the frozen area is white, as the pigment forming cells have been destroyed, and the cow is num-

A cow that has been freeze branded

bered for life. If the cow has an all-white rump, a second application of the iron is made to destroy the hair follicles. This leaves the number as a bald path and some permanent damage is caused to the hide.

Calf rearing

As soon as a calf is born, the mother licks it thoroughly all over with her strong, rough tongue. The calf is stimulated by this action and it is soon on its feet seeking its mother's teats for a first vital feed of colostrum.

Dairy calves are removed from their dams after this feed and put into individual pens in a warm, dry and well-ventilated house. Individual penning is necessary for correct feeding and to prevent navel sucking. Navel sucking by calves can lead to infection in one calf and balls of hair in the stomach of the other.

The photograph shows that each calf has two buckets: one is for clean water and the other is for palatable nutritious calf food in the form of small pellets. Pellets, water and hay are always on offer.

In addition, two daily feeds of milk are given from a sterile bucket, consisting of 2.5 litres of feed made by mixing milk powder with warm water. The calf is weaned from milk at about six weeks old and other foods are introduced (mangels, beet pulp, and so on.) also at this time the calf pellets are gradually replaced with cheaper rearing nuts.

In practice, there is much more skill in calf-rearing than the account suggests. Baby calves are delicate, can easily become ill and the strictest hygiene is necessary to prevent cross-infection.

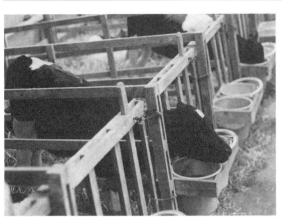

Calves in pens

Thorough cleansing of premises and utensils must be carried out between successive batches of calves. Sick calves usually 'scour' (have diarrhoea), and when this happens the cause *must* be found or death soon occurs.

Calves bought in a market often scour due to the shock of movement. It is standard practice to feed bought in calves with glucose and warm water instead of milk for the first day or so.

Dehorning

Horned breeds are dehorned during the first few weeks of life. The calf is given a local anaesthetic and the horn buds removed with an electrically heated metal ring; the heat seals the blood vessels and prevents infection. Dehorned animals are much quieter and can be housed more intensively than horned cattle.

Bacteria and the dairy cow

Experiment 7.1

1. Take a bottle of fresh pasteurised or sterilised milk.
2. Divide the milk into two sterile stoppered bottles.
3. Into one bottle introduce 5 ml of topsoil.
4. Into the other bottle introduce 5 ml of top soil that has been sterilised by baking in an oven (at 110°C) for one hour:
5. Leave the bottles in a warm room, examine and smell daily.
6. Record your observations.

One bottle sours much more quickly than the other; why is this? ...Q.11

In the above experiment scouring was detected in a crude, inaccurate way.

Experiment 7.2

A more precise measurement of the keeping quality of milk (i.e. counting the number of bacteria present) is obtained with the resazurin test. Resazurin is a dye which colours milk blue. As the milk turns sour the colour changes to pink and further souring turns the sample white.

1. Obtain two different samples of milk: either pasteurised, raw, one day old, two days old, or milk from two different suppliers.
2. Dissolve a tablet of resazurin in 50 ml distilled water.
3. Place 10 ml of each sample in sterile tubes and 10 ml of fresh boiled milk in a third tube as a control.
4. Add 1 ml of resazurin to each tube and seal with a sterile bung.
5. Mix by inverting the tubes once.
6. Incubate the tubes in a water bath set at 37°C.
7. Observe the tubes at regular 10 minute intervals and note the time each takes to turn pink and then white.

Why were the samples kept at 37°C? ...Q.12

The dairy farmer has to observe strict hygiene to keep the numbers of bacteria in his milk at a low level. The milking machine and all milk pipes are thoroughly cleaned after each milking by circulating sterilising chemical solutions. Cows' udders and teats are washed before milking and dried with a disposable paper towel to prevent passing bacteria from cow to cow. The milk is cooled as rapidly as possible to slow the growth of any bacteria present.

The effect of temperature on bacteria growth in milk

Temperature at which milk is kept (°C)	Number of bacteria present per ml of milk		
	Fresh	24 hours later	48 hours later
5	4000	4000	4200
10	4000	13 000	120 000
15	4000	1 500 000	32 000 000

Not all bacteria are outside the cow; some enter the udder through the teat and multiply rapidly:

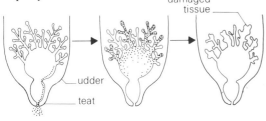

bacteria enter through teat canal

clinical mastitis follows: swollen, painful udder, clots and blood in the milk

mammary tissue left is damaged, reducing cow's ability to produce milk

Mastitis

Bacteria in the udder cause inflammation and swelling – a condition known as mastitis. Very often mastitis is sub-clinical (there are no external symptoms) and the farmer is unaware of its presence. Sub-clinical mastitis reduces milk yield but can be detected by counting the number of cells per ml of milk. Cell counts are taken in the laboratories of the Milk Marketing Board and the farmer is informed.

Number of cells per ml of milk	Mastitis problem	Milk lost per cow per year (litres)
250 000–500 000	Slight	170
500 000–750 000	Average	300
Over 750 000	Bad	700

The cells are dead white blood cells which have left the bloodstream to engulf the invading bacteria. The incidence of sub-clinical mastitis is very much reduced if the teats are dipped in iodine solution after each milking:

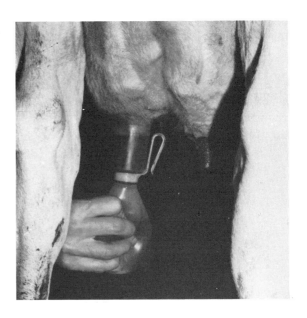

Clinical mastitis results from different bacteria entering the udder and multiplying rapidly, causing clots in the milk and inflammation and swelling of the mammary tissue. This type of mastitis the farmer can see and, in order to detect it in the early stages, he draws the foremilk from each teat into a strip cup that has a black plate fitted to show any clots.

Clinical mastitis is treated by squeezing a tube of antibiotic through the teat orifice; these are obtained from a vet and his instructions must be strictly followed or resistant strains of bacteria may be bred.

The life of the dairy animal

The majority of dairy calves are born in the autumn, and their mothers will then produce milk in winter when the price (to farmers) is high.

The calf is allowed to suckle its mother to obtain a first vital feed of colostrum and is carried away to an individual pen in the calf house with a warm bed of straw. It can smell and see the other calves all lying comfortably in the airy, insulated shed.

Later, buckets of milk are brought in, one for each calf. The new calf does not know how to drink and keeps raising its head to find its mother's teats. The calf-rearer dips his/her hand in the warm milk, allows the calf to suck the fingers and gently forces the calf's head into the bucket.

During the next six weeks milk feeds are given twice daily in addition to hay, water and pellets, which the calves enjoy chewing. When the calf is eating almost a kilo of pellets a day its milk feeds are stopped.

The calf is moved into a large pen with other heifers who feed and lie together. In May the calves are turned out and live entirely on grass until December when hay is placed in racks in the field.

The following summer the heifers grow rapidly on grass and, in October, an Aberdeen Angus bull is introduced, to mate with them. They spend a second winter outside. The following June the heifers join the dairy herd and learn the twice daily routine of leaving the fields and passing through the milking parlour. The heifers are soon as eager as the cows to enter the parlour where they receive a steaming up ration of cake.

During August the heifers calve and begin to produce milk. On a certain day each week the milk is weighed and the rations adjusted according to yield. Three or four months later the heifers become pregnant once more, this time as a result of artificial insemination. No longer is the winter spent outside, but in the large, warm covered yard.

The heifers continue milking until the end of June when yields fall rapidly and they become dry, giving no milk at all. The heifers (now cows) calve in September and the milking routine restarts. Each subsequent year the cows produce a calf and milk for about ten months followed by two months rest. After four or five lactations the cows are allowed to become barren (not in calf) and are sold.

Individual cows are capable of producing ten or more calves. In practice farmers maintain young herds as they give better quality milk and have less mastitis and disease problems.

How old is a heifer when she produces her first calf? ...Q.13
What colour are the first calves if the heifers are Friesians? ...Q.14
Why should a calf suckle its mother before being taken to the rearing house? ...Q.15

A herd of beef cattle on chalk downland

The life of the beef animal

The calf intended for beef is reared in one of three ways:

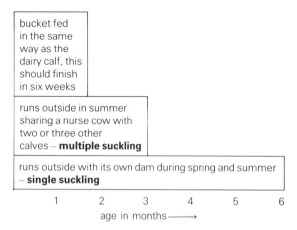

The reared calf is finished in one of three ways:

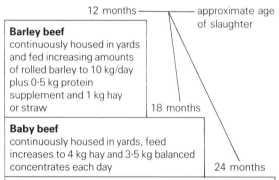

Male calves are usually castrated, after which they are called *bullocks*. Bullocks grow larger than heifers and are often kept longer as they do not begin to store fat until they are older.

Beef animals are slaughtered before they are fully grown; the usual slaughter weight is 400–500 kg on the hoof. Many beef animals are sold by auction; the animal is weighed as it enters the sale ring and buyers bid in pence per kg.

The biology of the ox

A healthy cow at rest; respiration rate 12–16 per minute; pulse rate 45–50 per minute; temperature 39°C.

What effect would galloping across a field have on these three rates? ...Q.16

Gestation period 283 days; oestrus one day every three weeks.

The reproductive system, the respiratory system and the circulatory system of the ox are similar to those of the pig. Refer to *GCSE Rural Science 1* to revise them.

The digestive system is similar to that of other ruminants and is described in Chapter 6 of this book.

Dentition

The dental formula of the ox is:

$$i \frac{0-0}{4-4} \quad c \frac{0-0}{0-0} \quad pm \frac{3-3}{3-3} \quad m \frac{3-3}{3-3}$$

The only teeth the animal has in the upper jaw are molars; the lower jaw has eight incisors which bite against a hard pad in the top jaw – as shown in the photograph:

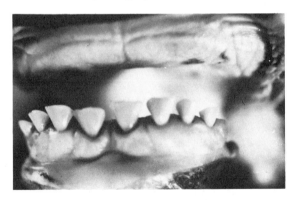

Which type of teeth are completely absent in the ox? ...Q.17

Examination of a cow's head shows that the molars in the bottom jaw cannot meet the molars in the top jaw as this jaw is somewhat wider.

Observation of a ruminating cow shows that the bottom jaw is moving from side to side and not up and down.

This sideways movement would quickly wear the molars of many mammals smooth, but the molars of the ox have alternate ridges of dentine and enamel; the softer dentine wears below the enamel which forms a permanently sharp cutting edge.

Task 7.7

softer dentine wears lower than enamel keeping the tooth permanently sharp

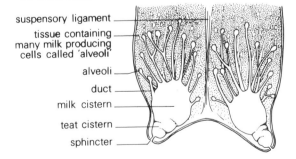

new molar **worn molar**

Copy the diagrams above and use different colours to show the enamel, dentine and pulp.

Milk secretion

Milk is produced in the cow's mammary gland which is usually called the udder. The udder is divided into four separate quarters, each having its own teat:

- suspensory ligament
- tissue containing many milk producing cells called 'alveoli'
- alveoli
- duct
- milk cistern
- teat cistern
- sphincter

The udder contains millions of tiny pockets (alveoli) surrounded with milk-secreting cells. The alveoli are connected by a network of converging ducts to cavity (milk cistern) at the base of the udder, which connects to the teat cistern. The base of the teat is kept closed by a sphincter muscle – a circular muscle which closes a tube.

Milk secretion begins with the birth of a calf and is a continuous process; the cells around the alveoli remove substances from the cow's blood and convert them to milk. The milk is passed to the alveoli where it is stored, and secretion slows as pressure in the alveoli increases.

As the presence of a lot of milk in the udder reduces the rate at which it is made, dairy cows are milked twice a day with the interval between milkings as near to 12 hours as possible.

The substances which are converted into milk are carried in the blood to the udder by two arteries. The large amount of blood flowing through the udder leaves via the 'milk vein' which can be seen under the skin of the cow's belly. A large milk vein is evidence that an animal is capable of high milk yields:

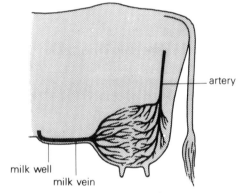

Milk let down

Before milk can be removed from the udder it must be released from the alveoli and adjoining ducts and allowed to flow to the teat. The release of milk from mammary tissue to teat is known as 'let down':

In the diagram:

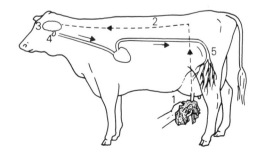

1. The teat is stimulated by the sucking calf.
2. A message travels via a nerve from teat to brain.
3. The brain sends a message to the pituitary gland which is situated just below.
4. The pituitary gland responds by producing a hormone called oxytocin and discharging it into the blood stream.
5. A minute or so later the hormone reaches the udder, and causes tiny muscles around the alveoli to contract, forcing the milk in the direction of the teat.
6. The calf continues to drink for about eight minutes after which the effect of the hormone wears off.

In order to milk a cow, the farmer, not the sucking calf, must stimulate the production of oxytocin. He does this by washing the udder and teats whilst the animals is quietly eating her ration of cake.

A frightened cow produces a hormone called adrenalin which prevents let down of milk. A strange person walking around at milking time could frighten the cows and prevent milk let down. It is for this reason that farmers are reluctant to allow classes of children around at milking time and not because they are unfriendly.

A calf is born with teeth; how does it manage to suckle without hurting the teat, frightening the cow and preventing let down? ...Q.18

Pests and diseases of cattle

1. Diseases caused by parasites

Ringworm
Ringworm (*Trichophyton verrucosum*) is a parasitic fungus that can be transmitted to man.

The fungus grows in surface layers of skin, causing the hair to fall and a considerable amount of irritation. It is common in young animals in winter and early spring, and severe infections cause loss of condition. The fungus produces spores which can infect horses, dogs, pigs, sheep and goats. Ringworm is quickly cured by adding a substance called griseofulvin to the diet.

Husk
Caused by a nematode (*Dictyocaulus viviparus*) in the lungs. The males are 40 mm long and the females 70 mm; they live in the lungs of cattle, feeding on the delicate tissues. After mating, eggs are laid in the lungs. The larvae hatch and climb the trachea, and are swallowed but remain unharmed by the digestive juices so they pass out with the faeces.

Outside the cow, the larvae moult twice and form cysts that can live on pasture throughout the winter. If the cysts are eaten by cattle they develop in the intestines and migrate to the lungs:

Symptoms: Infected cattle develop a continual 'husky' cough and death may follow, especially in calves.

Treatment: Worms can be killed by various drugs but no drug will repair damaged lung tissue. Prevention is the most effective way of dealing with husk. A vaccine called Dictol given to calves before they are turned out to grass stimulates the calves' natural defence against these parasites and prevents them from migrating to the lungs.

Prevention can also be affected by good husbandry, by not overstocking pastures, moving

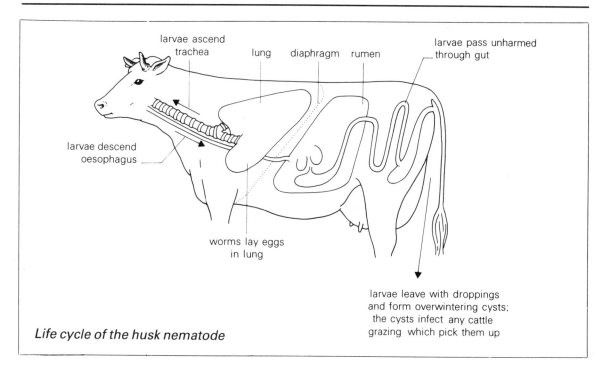

Life cycle of the husk nematode

young stock to fresh pasture in July and 'resting' closely-grazed pasture by taking a hay or silage crop.

Warble-fly (Hypoderma bovis)
In late winter swellings may appear on the backs of cattle and grow to the size of a small walnut. A fat grub, about 30 mm long, can be squeezed from each swelling; this grub is the larva of the warble-fly.

Life cycle (see also page 138):
The warble-fly lays its eggs from May to August on the legs of cattle, attaching them to individual hairs by small claspers.

Three to six days later a small larva emerges from the egg and bores through the skin. Once under the skin the larva migrates to the gullet of the cow where it forms a cyst. In February, the larva leaves the cyst and migrates through the spinal cord to the muscle on the cow's back. Here it feeds on the fluid produced by the inflamed flesh and bores a breathing hole through the skin.

During April the larva enlarges its breathing hole and emerges, falling to the ground. The creamy white larva changes to a somewhat smaller black pupa. Four weeks later the pupa hatches into an adult fly.

Damage:
1. Warble holes in the skin are repaired only with scar tissue. The scars are in the area which produces the best leather and they seriously reduce the value of the hide.
2. Valuable meat is made unfit for human consumption.
3. Animals which are host to warble-fly larva suffer great discomfort, lose condition and become less productive.

How can a beef animal become less productive?
...Q.19

4. Adult flies cause cattle to run wildly with their tails in the air; farmers call this behaviour 'gadding' and refer to the warble-fly as the gad-fly. Gadding can reduce milk yields by up to 25%.

Control: A single dressing of systemic insecticide poured on the back of the cow in October will

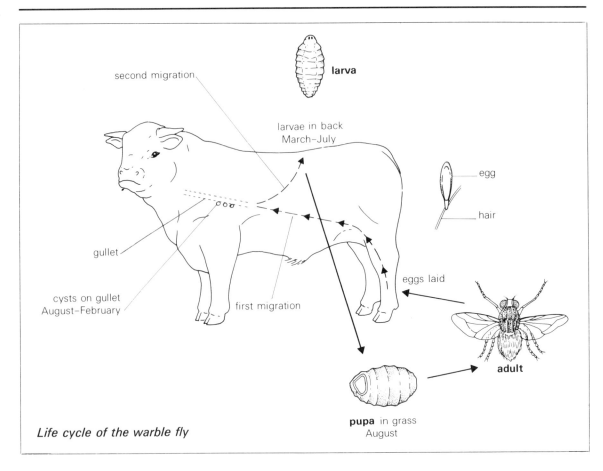

Life cycle of the warble fly

Cattle gadding

kill most of the warble-fly larvae in her body. If treatment is delayed until after November migrating larvae may be killed in the spine, causing paralysis in the animal. Full-sized larvae are killed in April and May by pouring insecticide on the backs of the cattle. Government orders compelling farmers to treat cattle for warble-fly are in force and it is hoped that the United Kingdom is now free of this pest.

The systemic insecticides used take about six hours to percolate the body. Therefore dairy cattle must not be treated during the six hours before milking or the milk could become contaminated.

2. Other diseases

Milk fever

Not all cattle illness is caused by parasites; milk fever is an example of a disorder of the metabolism.

Symptoms: A freshly-calved cow staggers, loses balance, falls down and is unable to rise. The body temperature falls four or five degrees below normal, breathing becomes slow and the pulse fast but weak. If left untreated the animal will most likely die.

Causes: The start of milk production causes the calcium level in the blood to fall rapidly and the animal is unable to replace it quickly enough. Normally the cow replaces the calcium in her milk from her food; the upset of having a calf sometimes causes the calcium replacement mechanism to fail and milk fever results.

Treatment: Half a litre of calcium borogluconate solution injected subcutaneously (underneath the skin) replaces the lost calcium and the animal is usually back on her feet in a few hours.

Task 7.8

Study the following list of cattle disorders and causes. Rewrite the words in two vertical columns with the correct cause against each disorder

foot and mouth disease	nematode
mastitis	virus
milk fever	fungus
warble-fly	bacteria
tuberculosis	metabolic disorder
ringworm	bacteria
husk	insect

Questions: Cattle

1. Write single sentences to answer the following questions:
   (a) What is meant by artificial insemination?
   (b) How does milk from a Jersey cow differ from the milk from a Friesian cow?
   (c) How much butter is made from one litre of milk?
   (d) What animal was killed in Poland in 1627?
   (e) Why were Charolais cattle bred to have large hind quarters?
   (f) Why are attempts being made to save rare breeds?
   (g) How can a freeze brand be applied to an all white animal?
   (h) Why are cattle dehorned?
   (i) What effect does the hormone oxytocin have in cattle?
   (j) Which pest of cattle is hopefully now extinct in the UK?
   (k) How is the volume of milk measured in a bulk tank?

2. (a) An animal which chews its cud is called a ruminant. In the rumen live organisms which feed upon the host's food and make the digestion of cellulose possible. Fatty acids and large quantities of gas are produced in the rumen.
   (i) Describe how an animal chews its cud.
   (ii) What is cellulose?
   (iii) What happens either to the gas or to the fatty acids which are produced in the rumen?
   (iv) Name one type of organism which lives in the rumen.
   (v) A ruminant spends a lot of time chewing grass which contains hard substances. Why do the molar teeth

not wear smooth?
(b) Describe the importance of the ruminant in the food chains which end with humans.

3. Outline the way in which you would care for a milking animal through a one-year period.
   Mention in your answer: housing; summer feeding; winter feeding; milking; bedding; grooming; hygiene.

4. The Milk Marketing Board operate an artificial insemination service.
   (a) Describe the collection and storage of semen.
   (b) Explain how the semen is implanted in the female.
   (c) List the advantages this service gives to the dairy farmer.
   (d) What long term effects is this service likely to have upon the national herd?

5. A dairy farmer feeds his cattle 1 kg of hay plus 5 kg of mangels for each 50 kg body weight for their maintenance ration. In addition he feeds a production ration of 1 kg of concentrates for each 5 litres of milk a cow produces.
   What rations will each of the following cows receive?:
   (a) A 500 kg cow giving 20 litres of milk.
   (b) A 450 kg dry cow.
   (c) A 550 kg cow giving 35 litres of milk.
   (d) A 550 kg cow giving 10 litres of milk.
   (e) A 400 kg cow giving 40 litres of milk.

6. (a) What is meant by the term 'pedigree' in livestock breeding?
   (b) Describe how a non-pedigree herd of Friesians can be graded up to pedigree status.
   (c) Why is it not possible to grade up a non-pedigree herd of Herefords to pedigree status?
   (d) In what ways have the Herd Societies improved the quality of cattle in this country?

7. In the milking parlour hygiene is of extreme importance.
   (a) Explain why poor hygiene causes milk to turn sour.
   (b) Explain why poor hygiene increases the mastitis problem in a dairy herd.
   (c) Describe in detail how the incidence of mastitis can be reduced in a dairy herd.

8. Scientific research has made possible:
   (a) An increase in the numbers of eggs a cow produces during one heat period.
   (b) The removal of fertilised embryos from a cow's uterus.
   (c) The storage of living embryos for long periods.
   (d) The implantation of a fertilised embryo into another cow, in such a way that a normal pregnancy results.
   Describe how these advances are now being used to improve cattle breeding around the world.

9. (a) Name two breeds of beef cattle, one a native breed and the other imported from the mainland of Europe.
   (b) In what ways are the breeds you have named
      (i) similar?
      (ii) different?
   (c) Describe how beef cattle are raised on a hill farm by the single suckling method and contrast this with barley beef production on a lowland farm.

8 Intensive poultry production

Broilers

A broiler is a chicken which is intensively-reared (a large number in a small area) for the table and sold as an oven-ready bird either fresh-chilled or frozen.

The broiler industry is big business as over 350 million are eaten in Britain each year. Scientific breeding and nutrition coupled with large-scale production has reduced the price of chicken, making it cheap compared with red meat. Labour costs are also low as one person can care for as many as 70 000 birds.

Task 8.1

Visit a supermarket or butcher's shop and obtain the price (per kg) of the following: topside, chine, pork leg, chicken, lamb leg and lamb shoulder. Plot these prices on a histogram for easy comparison.

Cattle concentrates and broiler food are made from the same ingredients; why is beef so much more expensive than chicken? ...Q.1

The stock

Chickens grown as broilers are different from chickens grown to produce eggs. All broiler chicks are hybrids, produced from foundation stock of White Rocks, White Cornish, and a few other breeds. The following points are bred for:

*Good feed conversion ratio.
*White feathers and flesh.
*Rapid growth.
*Docile temperament.
*High resistance to disease.
*Good carcase shape with a high proportion of breast meat.
*Similarity between the sexes.
*Quick feathering (a breed which feathers quickly will require less heat and be less prone to cannibalism).

The unit

A modern broiler unit is run by two persons and consists of four houses each having a floor area of 2000 m². The owners probably have a number of similar units in different areas.

Why are the units not all on the same site? ...Q.2

Each house is specially constructed and designed to control the environment inside:
A controlled environment poultry house is a low building without windows, air being admitted or expelled through baffled openings on the ridge and on the sides. The following environmental factors are controlled:

1. Day length
2. Light intensity
3. Temperature
4. Ventilation

Why are there no windows in a controlled environment house? ...Q.3

Exterior view of a broiler house

1. *Day length*

To encourage the birds to a high food intake, electric lights are kept on for twenty-three hours each day. Some growers leave the lights on continuously; a power failure would panic these birds as they become unaccustomed to the dark.

2. *Light intensity*

For the first few days of the chickens' lives the lights are kept bright (10–20 lux) to encourage them to eat and drink. Light intensity is gradually reduced to a low level (2 lux) when the birds are feeding well. Birds are less active at a low light intensity and therefore grow better using less energy for activity. Feather pecking – birds pecking each others' feathers, a vice which can lead to cannabalism – is much less likely to occur when lighting is low.

3. *Temperature*

Temperature is an important environmental factor, especially during the first weeks when the chickens are not properly feathered. To minimise heat loss the walls and roof of broiler houses are double skinned and packed with insulating material like fibre glass or polystyrene.

Heat is supplied by electric, gas or oil heaters inside, which raises the temperature of the whole

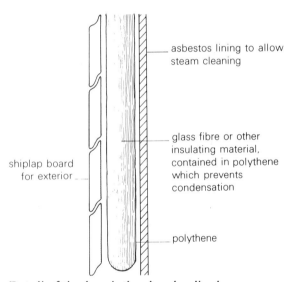

Detail of the insulation in a broiler house

house to 30°C when the birds first arrive. During the next three weeks the temperature is gradually reduced to 21°C. Some houses have brooders, which heat small areas only to these temperatures, and the birds are confined in groups of 3000 to the warm areas during the first two weeks.

4. *Ventilation*

In summer the temperature can be reduced if necessary by increasing ventilation. The purpose of ventilation is to introduce fresh air, remove

Intensive poultry production   143

waste gases and moisture, and maintain a uniform environment unaffected by outside weather conditions. The rate of ventilation is expressed in cubic metres of air per second per tonne of food consumed each day. In order to have sufficient control of ventilation there must be enough fans to vary the rate from two to twenty-four, according to conditions.

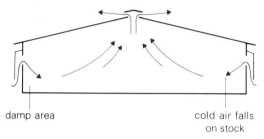

Section through a broiler house showing natural ventilation

Warm air A rises and leaves through the ridge outlet; air is replaced by cold air which enters through the side ventilators and falls onto the stock. This air flow chills the stock and creates wet patches of litter around the walls. Damp helps the spread of coccidiosis and other diseases.

Name another animal in addition to the chicken which contracts coccidiosis.   ...Q.4

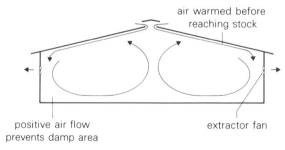

Section through a broiler house showing the air flow with a fan controlled ventilation

Here the flow is reversed with air brought in through the ridge and held to the ceiling by maintaining a speed of 5 m/sec. It is warmed before falling near to the walls and over the chickens. The positive air flow at the sides of the building prevents the formation of damp patches in the litter. This type of ventilation is least affected by wind and outside conditions.

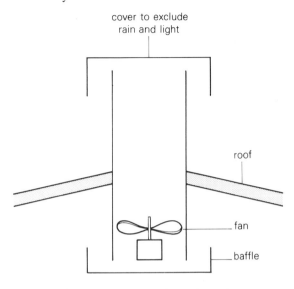

Detail of the air inlet on the ridge of a controlled environment broiler house

View of the interior of a broiler house showing extraction fans

The life of the broiler chicken

The broilers' life begins on a tray in a large incubator. The birds are removed after a few hours and sexed, the pullets placed in one box and cockerels in another. Both sexes develop into table birds but to obtain the best results, the feeding programme for males needs to be a little different from the feeding programme for females.

The chickens are boxed and transported by insulated van to a broiler feeding unit. As many as 30 000 birds are put into a controlled environment house 100 m long and 20 m wide.

How many birds are there per m^2? ...Q.5

The house has been empty for almost three weeks during which time it has been thoroughly cleaned and disinfected by a specialist firm of contractors. It is also warm as the heaters have been running for the previous 24 hours. The floor is covered with chopped straw to a depth of 100 mm. Bacteria in the straw make short work of the droppings, producing ammonia gas which is removed by the controlled ventilation.

The chickens begin to feed on broiler crumbs and drink from the conical drinkers as soon as they find them; this does not take long as both food and water are available in all parts of the house at less than three metres' working distance.

Broilers do not wander about but remain in the same area with the birds they can recognise; they soon learn which chicks to avoid – and which they can peck without fear of retaliation. Not that they do much pecking because, after two days, the lights dim and, apart from eating and drinking during their twenty-three hour day, they are fairly inactive.

They are never short of food as a chain moves slowly along the bottom of the continuous troughs dragging food with it from the huge bulk hopper at the end of the building. Two or three times each day someone in sterile clothing checks the birds and reads the instruments which are recording temperature and humidity.

The broilers grow quickly, and there seems to be less space each day, as the bodies grow and feathers develop. Wing and tail feathers grow during the first few days and, by the end of three weeks, feathering is almost complete. During the eight weeks spent in the house the broilers eat just over 4 kg of food each and grow to a liveweight of almost exactly 2 kg. They are then removed and taken to a packing station to be prepared as oven-ready birds, weighing about 1600 g. It takes two or three days to catch and crate 30 000 birds, the actual time depending upon the capacity of the packing station.

Broilers – facts and figures

* Broiler food is high in energy and protein and is compounded from wheat, maize, fish meal, meat meal with added fat, vitamins and minerals.
* Rations change twice during the growing period getting progressively lower in protein.
* Drugs are added to feed to speed growth and control disease.
* Very high food conversion rates of 2.2:1 are achieved. If birds are grown larger than 2 kg the food conversion rate falls.
* Average flock mortality is 4%.
* A typical production cycle for 2 kg live weight birds is 73 days, 55 days growing the chicks and 18 days cleaning the house ready for the next batch.

How many broilers can be produced in a single shed, with a capacity of 30 000, during one year, ignoring mortality? ...Q.6

* 1000 broilers require eight circular drinkers and 25 metres of trough space.

The peck order

In natural conditions animals of the same species often fight but never kill each other. One animal in the fight submits and the winner stops fighting. However when kept in intensive conditions birds often kill each other and cannibalism can cause serious losses both on deep litter and in multiple bird cages.

A group of birds soon learn to recognise each other and establish a 'peck order'. After a number of encounters between two birds, each will know which one is master. After that, the one will always give way to the other, for example moving away from the feed troughs, and the master bird knows that it can peck without fear of retaliation. In small flocks, each bird soon learns its position in the peck order which may be linear: bird 1 can peck all the others; bird 2 can peck all the others except bird 1; bird 3 can peck all the others except 1 and 2; bird 4 can peck all the others except 1, 2 and 3 and so on.

In practice, the peck order is seldom as simple as this. It could be that bird 2 can peck all the others except bird 3; and bird 3 cannot peck birds 1 and 4 but can peck all others in the flock. The last few birds in the peck order are very underprivileged. They have more difficulty in obtaining food and will perform less well than they should.

A bird cannot recognise more than about 30 individuals so in a large house the birds form sub-flocks, of about this number, which stay in one defined area. If there are enough food and water troughs spaced to allow these sub-flocks to feed without straying into other sub-flock territory the possibility of fights and cannibalism will be much reduced.

Egg production

Battery cages

There are over 50 million laying fowl in Britain and 45 million of these are kept in battery cages. Battery cages are housed in controlled environment houses, similar to those described for broilers except that they are a little higher so as to house three or four tiers of cages – just over two metres at the ridge.

Much of the UK egg production has left the general farm, and birds are kept in specialist units of 20 000 and more.

A single battery cage is made of galvanised steel wires welded together, to form sections. The sections are fitted together to make a cage. The front of the cage has wide bars through which the bird can put its head in order to feed. The floor slopes towards the front to allow eggs to roll outside the cage where they can be collected. The mesh of the floor is large enough to allow droppings to fall through as they are produced.

At the back of the cage is a nipple drinker,

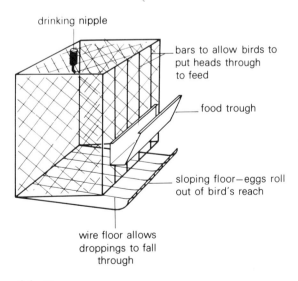

A battery cage

A block of battery cages

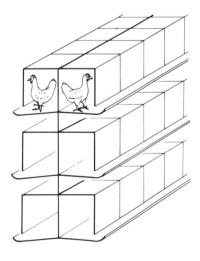

similar to the one described for rabbits in Book 2. The drinker is placed at the back of the cage so it can be shared by birds in the adjoining cage which faces in the opposite direction.

The cages are arranged in tiers of three or four, usually with two rows back to back. The tiers are repeated, forming blocks of cages which run the length of the house.

There are many systems for removing the droppings, the most common of which is a sheet of tough plastic laid under the cages. Each day an electric motor moves the sheet along like a conveyor belt and the droppings are turned on to another belt, which removes them from the house. Droppings are used as fertiliser or are dried and included in rations for ruminants.

Cages vary in size; an average size is 600 mm × 400 mm × 450 mm high and a cage of this size would house four birds.

Task 8.2

1. Cut a piece of card 60 cm by 40 cm – the size of a battery cage floor.
2. Measure the length and width of a fully grown hen.
3. View the bird from directly above; draw a full size outline.
4. Cut four templates to fit your outline.
5. Spread the templates on your rectangular card, can you make them fit? That is all the space the birds have and remember they also have wings.

If battery cages became illegal eggs would possibly cost a few more pence a dozen. Would *you* mind paying the extra? Write an account explaining why battery cages should (or should not) be made illegal.

The deep litter system

Another method of housing laying birds is the deep litter system. Although little used for commercial layers, almost all breeding stock are housed in this way. Instead of the controlled environment house being filled with battery

Birds in a battery cage

cages the floor is covered with straw, wood shavings or peat to a depth of 250 mm and the birds live on top of this. Normal stocking density is four birds per 1 m^2. The Code of Recommendations for the welfare of domestic fowls specifies 14.7 kg of birds per 1 m^2.

A communal nest box

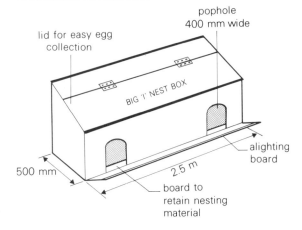

Heating is not provided in deep litter houses but there is good insulation, for the warmth of the birds and bacterial activity in the litter is usually sufficient to maintain the temperature above 10°C. Below this temperature the bacteria work too slowly to break down the droppings, and the litter becomes wet and soiled.

As well as food troughs and water drinkers, nest boxes are provided. These are usually of the communal type shown in the diagram; the sloping top prevents the boxes from being used as a roost.

Why are birds prevented from roosting on the nest boxes? ...Q.7

The nest box is usually lined with hay or sawdust and a box is provided for every 50 birds.

One problem experienced with the deep litter system is that birds sometimes go broody and stop laying. These birds spend almost all their time in the nest boxes but an experienced person can easily spot them. The broody bird can be brought back into production by being placed in a wire-floored coop with ad lib food and water for three days.

Advantages and disadvantages of the deep litter system over the battery cage system

Disadvantages

1. Higher labour costs. One person can look after only about 5000 layers.
2. Less birds in the controlled environment house.
3. More skill required.
4. Parasitic diseases spread more rapidly.
5. Cost of litter.

Advantages

1. Problem of manure disposal only arises once a year.
2. The building can be put to other uses.
3. No cages to purchase.

Free range

Birds can be kept in small houses and allowed to range in the fields during the day. This system is known as free range and is uneconomic for the following reasons:

1. A large area of land is required.
2. It is not possible to control the lighting pattern and egg production in winter is low.
3. A large amount of labour is required.

Lighting for egg production

Increasing day length acts on a bird's brain and causes the release of hormones, and these stimulate egg laying:
In nature birds lay in spring when the day length is increasing and they are unlikely to lay during autumn, when daylength is decreasing. In addition, birds lay more eggs when days are long and less eggs when days are short.

The intensity (brightness) of the light also has an effect on production; bright light (up to a maximum of 50 lux) encourages egg laying and dim light discourages egg laying.

Farmers make use of these facts and adjust their lighting programmes to obtain maximum production. If the farmer is to have complete control over this part of the environment he must exclude daylight as this can be variable in

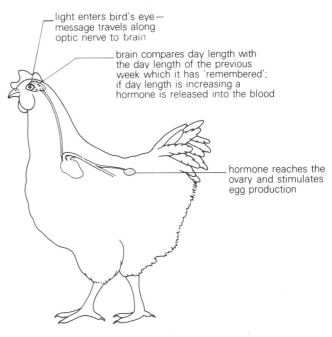

intensity and he may want to have his 'days' shorter than the outside daylight. For this reason laying houses have no windows and the air intakes are baffled with black polythene to exclude all natural light. Natural daylight varies like this: ——————

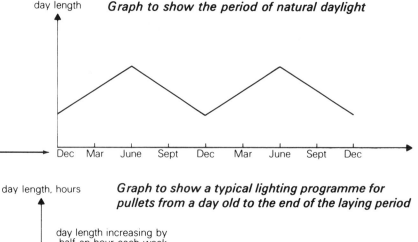

Graph to show the period of natural daylight

Lights are switched on and off by electric time switches, adjusted each week to give the desired increase or decrease. Stepping the lights down during the rearing period delays the sexual maturity of the birds, making them larger in size when they first begin to lay. Birds reared on this pattern lay less small eggs than those reared with longer days.

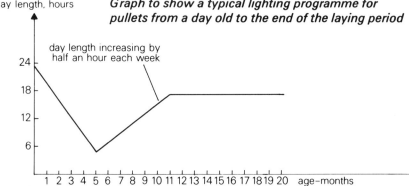

Graph to show a typical lighting programme for pullets from a day old to the end of the laying period

Suggest another advantage of having a six hour day when the pullets first begin to lay. ...Q.8

Although the farmer has no problems with adjusting the length of the birds' day for maximum production, he has considerable difficulty in adjusting the light intensity as bright lights and varying intensities have side effects:

1. The brighter the lights the greater the electricity bill.
2. The brighter the lights the greater the possibility of cannibalism.
3. Shadow in deep litter houses cause the birds to lay there instead of in the nests.
4. If some food troughs are more brightly lit than others birds fight over these and ignore the dimly-lit ones.

Red light does not reduce the possibility of feather pecking and cannibalism. If white bulbs are replaced with red light intensity is reduced, which accounts for the reduction in activity.

On large units where a light intensity of 25 lux is used the cost of electricity per bird in one year is roughly equal to the price of one egg.

Food for laying stock

The bird requires food for: growth (laying birds grow slowly until they are 45 weeks old), body maintenance, and egg production.

Large birds need more food per day than small birds. Food for layers is always on offer and the birds usually take only the food they need. Some large birds may overeat towards the end of the laying period and become fat. Laying birds housed inside are usually fed pellets which have been compounded from the following:

To provide protein	*To provide energy*
Fish meal	Maize
Meat meal	Wheat and wheat offals
Soya bean meal	Barley
Field beans	Oats
Sunflower meal	(Minerals)
	(Vitamins)

Birds on deep litter have limestone grit in hoppers which is essential for the formation of hard egg shells. But, if this grit is fed ad lib to birds in cages, they eat too much and their mineral balance is upset.

To each tonne of food for battery cage birds 75 kg of limestone flour is added to provide the calcium necessary for the formation of egg shells. In addition flint grit is fed once a month at the rate of 3 kg per 100 birds to maintain the gizzard in healthy condition.

Why does the gizzard need flint grit? ...Q.9

Eggs are 65% water and it is important that a constant supply of water is available. When pullets are put first into battery cages lights must be left bright until all the birds have learned how to obtain water from the nipple drinkers.

Breeds for egg production

There are many different hybrids suitable for egg production, each with the name given to it by the firm producing the bird. These hybrids are not simple first cross F_1 hybrids but are the result of computer-controlled breeding programmes involving several crosses. The birds available fall into two groups:

1. White feathered lightweight birds (1.7 kg) laying white eggs.
2. Brown feathered medium weight birds (2.0 kg) laying brown eggs.

The first group are based on various strains of White Leghorn and the second group are based on Rhode Island Red, Light Sussex and White Leghorn (see *Start Rural Science*).

The light hybrids lay more eggs and eat less food; in what ways are the light hybrids inferior to the heavy hybrids? ...Q.10

Measuring egg production

In order to compare the production of one pen of birds with another (which may contain a different number of birds) egg production is expressed as a percentage. The percentage production is calculated thus:

$$\frac{\text{number of eggs laid in one day}}{\text{number of birds housed}} \times \frac{100}{1}$$

For example, if 3000 birds were housed and some time later 2400 eggs were produced in a single day the percentage production would be:

$$\frac{2400}{3000} \times \frac{100}{1} = 80\%$$

If any birds die the number in the calculation is not adjusted as egg production is always calculated on the number of birds placed in the house and not the number actually there on any given day.

What would be the percentage egg production from a pen of birds laying 2920 eggs daily if 4000 birds were originally housed? ...Q.11

Comparison between light and heavy hybrids

	Weeks in production	Eggs laid per bird housed	Food consumption per bird per day (in grams)	Mortality %	EGGS Grade 1 & 2 %	Grade 3–7 %	Seconds %
Light hybrid	52	250	105	9	30	65	5
Heavy hybrid	52	240	135	9	50	45	5

Task 8.3

A flock of birds were placed in cages when they were 20 weeks old; the production during their year's laying period was as follows:

Age in weeks	20	24	28	32	36	40	44	48	52	56	60	64	68	72
Egg production (%)	0	20	70	90	90	85	80	78	75	72	70	65	60	55

Plot the production of this flock on a line graph, with percentage production on the vertical axis and age of birds along the horizontal axis.

The figures given in the task above are typical of the modern hybrid layer. Producers are not interested in the performance of individual birds but only in the performance of flocks. Depending upon the price of eggs, the money received when production fell to 55% would probably not cover the cost of the food consumed; the birds would then be replaced by a flock of pullets. Some growers force the laying flock to moult and keep them for a second laying season; it is more usual to replace laying birds after they have been laying for a year or just over.

Turkeys

Turkeys have a favourable meat/bone ratio and good food conversion rates. They reached this country from America, via Turkey, hence the name. Over the years the turkey has gradually replaced the goose as the traditional Christmas bird.

The old breeds of turkeys were bronze or black with a large pointed breastbone with very little flesh on it. These breeds have been abandoned, as white breeds give a much cleaner looking carcase. Selective breeding over the years has produced a bird with a broad breast, so broad in fact that natural mating has become almost impossible and breeding is achieved by artificial insemination of the hens housed in battery cages.

White turkeys

Breeds

A few years ago a number of turkey breeders pooled their resources and formed a group, British United Turkeys, with the aim of breeding the best possible type of bird. This venture was so successful that over 80% of Britain's turkeys are Triple 5 or Triple 6, which are the breeds of British United Turkeys. The Triple 5 is a small bird ideal for the family, and Triple 6 is a large bird grown for the hotel and catering trade.

Rearing turkeys

Turkeys intended for deep freezing or sale at low weights are kept in controlled environment houses in a similar way to broiler chickens with stags and hens housed separately. The hens reach 5 kg live weight at 15 weeks (food conversion rate 2.7) and the stags (males) reach 7 kg live weight (food conversion rate 2.5) at the same age.

Large birds are grown in cheaper types of houses with plenty of natural ventilation. Triple 6 stags reach live weights of 18 kg by 24 weeks. Large birds are much more costly to produce as the food conversion ratio (FCR) increases rapidly with age.

Age in weeks	Live-weight (kg)	Food consumed each week (kg)	Food conversion ratio for that week	Cumulative FCR
3	0.5	0.35	1.6	1.4
6	2.0	1.0	1.8	1.6
9	3.8	1.5	2.1	1.8
12	6.0	2.0	2.8	2.1
15	8.5	2.2	3.3	2.4
18	11.0	2.8	4.0	2.7
21	14.0	3.2	5.3	3.0
24	16.0	4.2	7.1	3.5

A poultry drinker – suitable for birds from a day old to adult

Detail of a poultry drinker

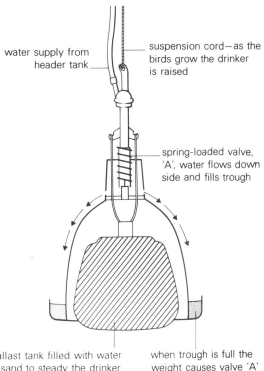

Questions: Intensive poultry production

1. Write single sentences to answer the following questions:
   (a) What is a broiler?
   (b) What three high protein foods are used in poultry rations?
   (c) What does 'ad lib' mean when it refers to feeding poultry?
   (d) Why are there no windows in an intensive laying house?
   (e) Which bird has the turkey replaced for the traditional Christmas dinner?
   (f) Which kind of bird is bred by artificial insemination?
   (g) What is the percentage production from a poultry flock of 1500 birds on a day when 1200 eggs are produced?

2. An agricultural research station kept batches of broilers in identical conditions but varied the stocking density of each house.

   Results

Stocking density	1	2	3	4	5	6	7	8
Profit per bird	10	14	17	22	27	25	13	9

   Note: stocking density in birds per sq. m *or* birds/m^2.
   profit in pence per bird.

   (a) Plot the figures on a graph and draw a line through the points.
   (b) Which stocking density gives the highest profit per bird?
   (c) Which stocking density would give the highest total profit?
   (d) Suggest a possible reason for the large drop in profit between a stocking density of 6 and a stocking density of 7.
   (e) How much profit would be made if 20 000 birds were kept at a stocking density of 5?

3. (a) Describe how large numbers of birds may be kept for egg laying without placing them in cages.
   (b) List the advantages and disadvantages this method has when compared with battery cages.
   (c) Make out a case either for or against the banning of battery cages by law.

4. (a) Draw diagrams to show alternative methods of ventilating an intensive poultry house.
   (b) What are the advantages and disadvantages of the two methods you have described?
   (c) Describe the changes which would take place in the atmosphere of a densely stocked broiler house if the power supply to the fans failed.

5. (a) What factors can be controlled in a controlled-environment poultry house?
   (b) By reference to a laying bird explain how the factors you have named will increase
      (i) her egg production;
      (ii) the profit she makes.

6. (a) With words and diagrams describe a nipple drinker suitable for fixing in a battery cage (refer to Chapter 6 in *GCSE Rural Science 1*).
   (b) What advantages has this drinker when compared with an open trough across the front of the cage?
   (c) In back to back battery cages, nipple drinkers are usually fitted at the back, rather than the front, of the cage. Suggest reasons for this.

7. (a) What do you understand by 'food conversion ratio' when the term is applied to a turkey?
   (b) Which is the better food conversion ratio, one of 3 or one of 4?
   (c) 150 turkeys weighed 900 kilos when slaughtered. If these birds had eaten 3150 kilos of food during their life what food conversion ratio had been achieved?

Answers to in-text questions

1. Botany

1. No; the size and shapes vary.

Task 1.6

Experiment 1 shows that plants lose water through their leaves.

Experiment 2 shows that leaves lose most water through their under surface.

Experiment 3 shows that the leaf contains air.

No conclusions can be drawn from Experiment 4 except that air can be blown out of the leaf by blowing into the petiole. This suggests a tube or interconnecting air space along the length of the petiole and into the leaf.

2. The water comes from the soil.
3. The carbon dioxide comes from the air.
4. Water has entered the egg in distilled water. Water has left the egg in the sugar solution.
5. Through the membrane.
6. Water moved from the weak to the strong solution.
7. If a different shoot were used the leaf area would be different and comparisons would not be valid.
8. A forced draught.
9. As the plant grows the pointer moves down.
10. Apparent growth.
11. Apparent growth.
12. Real growth.
13. Apparent growth.
14. 0.
15. Increase.
16. Very slight increase.
17. A very large increase.
18. Increases.

Investigation 1.5

Leaves with complicated shapes dry more quickly than simple shaped leaves. Loss of water from the blotting paper could be assessed by weighing on a sensitive balance at regular intervals.

19. The shapes could be weighed at regular intervals on a sensitive balance.
20. Oxygen.
21. Carbon dioxide.
22. 11 kg of nitrogen; 5.5 kg of phosphate; 5.5 kg of potash.

2. Herbicides

1. Too much spray would kill the crop.
2. Too little spray would be ineffective against many weeds.
3. Carrot fly would be encouraged by hand weeding. Disturbance causes a carrot smell which attracts the fly and soil disturbance gives an ideal place to lay eggs. The soil should be firmly trodden alongside the row after hand weeding.
4. (a) A seedling will lose its leaves and die.
   (b) An established perennial will lose its leaves which it will quickly replace using energy stored in underground parts.
5. MCPA will be carried down into the root which would normally be inaccessible without digging. The root may also be killed.

6. There will be a reduction in the numbers of other types of weeds and an increase in knot-grass and cleavers.
7. Too much simazine would probably kill the crop plant also; if the application is very heavy the simazine could persist until the following year making it impossible to grow any kind of crop from seeds.
8. The buds of dormant blackcurrant bushes are green and would be affected by the spray.
9. Complete cover is unnecessary as the chemical will be translocated throughout the plant from areas which receive it.

Task 2.2

Safety precautions when handling chemical sprays

1. Read and follow carefully the instructions on the label.
2. Wash off immediately any spray that falls on the skin.
3. Take care not to breathe any spray.
4. Never spray when the wind causes spray to drift.
5. Wash out and thoughtfully dispose of any containers.
6. Make sure all sprays are properly labelled.
7. Keep sprays under lock and key and away from children.
8. Make sure no spray will enter drainage water or waterways.
9. Carefully wash equipment after use.

3. Protected cultivation

1. Sparrows or other birds.
2. Protects the blooms from wind and storm damage.
3. Etiolated plants have long internodes.
4. Thin glazing bars allow more light into the greenhouse than thick glazing bars.
5. Aluminium is strong, light and maintenance free.
6. Wooden glazing bars are thick, wood requires treating with preservatives.
7. 300 m².

8. The single span greenhouse will admit most diffuse light.
9. No – the plants would receive much less light.

Task 3.1

	Advantage	Disadvantage
Glass	Good greenhouse effect Easy access Lasts for many years.	Easily broken Expensive Heavy (it could be argued that is an advantage – will not blow away).
Polythene	Poor greenhouse effect Will not shatter Cheap Light	Difficult access. In theory access is easy, just lift the side of the sheet. In practice once disturbed the sheet is very difficult to replace. Needs replacing every two years.

Task 3.2

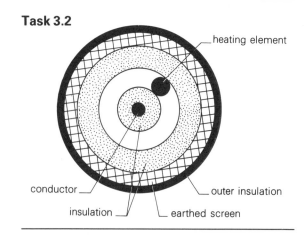

10. The bacteria which act upon ammonia are killed before the bacteria which produce it; the ammonia in the soil will increase – sometimes to a level which is harmful to seedlings.

11. Test the loam for pH.
12. 40 trays (the 10 litre box is filled 12 times making 120 litres of compost).
13. 20 trays (the 10 litre box is filled only four times when making seed compost).
14. Refer to the Glossary at the end of the book.
15. The tap water may be cold; water in a tank will be at greenhouse temperature.
16. John Innes No. 2 potting compost.
17. Cotyledon.
18. Wetting the greenhouse floor increases the humidity and reduces the plants' transpiration rate.
19. A minimum thermometer (or one side of a maximum and minimum thermometer).
20. If the flowers fail to set there will be no tomatoes.
21. Organisms of decay, mostly bacteria.
22. The fertilisers may enter the drainage water and eventually pollute a stream or river. Nitrogen causes excessive weed growth in streams; the organisms which decay the extra plant tissue remove oxygen from the water. Larger animals, e.g. fish, then die through lack of oxygen.
23. To prevent the growth of algae.
24. The willow.
25. The *Encarsia formosa* would all die and new introductions of whitefly would breed unchecked.
26. Four.
27. The longer day will prevent the females from hibernating and they will be removed with the drop debris in October.
28. The mite feeds upon red spiders.
29. Many red spiders are resistant to toxic chemicals.

4. Fruit

Task 4.1

Soft fruit: strawberry; loganberry: gooseberry; black currant; red currant; raspberry; blackberry.
Top fruit: apple; cherry; damson; pear; plum; peach.

1. Inside the fleshy parts.
2. Couch.
3. The plants will develop a good root system in the warm soil.
4. Strawberry pests and diseases are likely to be present in the soil of an old bed.
5. See Glossary.
6. Earthworms.
7. Lime.
8. The root system will not be disturbed.
9. Nitrogen.
10. Apply fertilisers or a good mulch of well-rotted manure.
11. The infected leaf has no cleft at the base, less notches up the sides and less veins.
12. Soil and climatic conditions.
13. Rootstocks grown from seed would not be true to type.
14. To prevent rusting.
15. 10.
16. Lodi, George Cave or Lord Lambourne.
17. To collect nectar and pollen.
18. By eating the bark from around the base.
19. Approximately 12%.
20. Pollinating insects would be killed.

Task 4.9

A scar on the fruit indicates sawfly.
The time of year, June for sawfly, later for codlining moth. Also (not in text) the saw fly larva has a distinctive noxious smell.

5. Gardens

1. Roses are the most important commercial flower in the UK.
2. Reducing the leaf area of the cutting reduces transpiration and therefore water stress and the cutting is more likely to root.
3. When the soil is dry enough to walk upon without poaching.
4. Ladybirds and their larvae feed upon aphids.
5. No – the mark is fairly random.
6. Most marks are continuous.
7. No – the mark tends to become wider.

8. Nothing is to be seen at the narrow end of the mark; a dark object can be seen at the wide end of the mark.
9. The palisade layer and the spongy tissue are missing and both upper and lower epidermis are intact.
10. Insect larva.
11. Insect pupa.
12. Good food supply; protection from predators; protection from dehydration. Cannot be washed or blown from the leaf.
13. Smaller than a housefly because the pupa is smaller.
14. Picking off and burning infected leaves.
15. The nematode causes a lot of damage because it is present in large numbers.
16. The bud will produce a shoot which will grow in the direction necessary to maintain the desired bush shape. An inward facing bud would probably produce a shoot which would grow into the centre of the bush.
17. A nymph is a young stage of an insect, resembling it in appearance except that it is smaller and sexually immature.
18. The use of a systemic insecticide.
19. The foam protects the nymph from predators; the foam protects the nymph from the possible harmful effects of sunshine.
20. Cereals are affected by rust diseases.
21. Photosynthesis.

6. Sheep

1. 24 kg.
2. Ridged fibres make stronger material than smooth fibres.
3. If the ewe gives a high yield the lamb will be well fed and grow quickly.
4. Seventeen days.
5. A creep is a barrier through which young animals can pass but not adults.
6. Cattle and goats are ruminants.
7. Absorption of fatty acids takes place through the rumen wall.
8. Foot and mouth disease.

7. Cattle

1. 300 kg.
2. Dairy farmers rear heifer calves to replace their cows as they become old; they use a dairy bull on their best milkers to provide these calves.
3. Aberdeen Angus calves have small heads and calvings are usually easy.
4. To produce calves for dairy herd replacement.
5. To produce calves which will make good beef animals.
6. No – she is on the B register.
7. Lacta.
8. Milked animals would become mixed with those still to be milked and would try to go through the parlour for a second time.
9. A Friesian requires more food than the Jersey for maintenance.
10. 6 kg.
11. The milk in the bottle to which the unsterilised soil was added would go sour first because of the bacteria in the soil.
12. To encourage the growth of bacteria and speed up the result.
13. Two years old.
14. Black – Aberdeen Angus bull black is dominant.
15. To obtain a feed of colostrum.
16. Respiration rate and pulse rate would increase, the temperature would remain the same.
17. Canine.
18. A calf has no incisors at the top, by putting out its tongue it covers its bottom teeth preventing them from biting the teat.
19. Grow less quickly.

Task 7.7

Foot and mouth – Virus
Mastitis – Bacteria
Milk fever – Metabolic disorder
Warble fly – Insect
Tuberculosis – Bacteria
Ringworm – Fungus
Husk – Nematode

8. Intensive poultry production

1. It takes almost 6 kg of food to provide 1 kg of beef and less than 3 kg of food to provide 1 kg of chicken.
2. Broiler units are scattered to reduce the spread of endemic diseases.
3. If windows were provided it would not be possible to control light intensity or day length.
4. Rabbit – see *GCSE Rural Science 1*.
5. 15 birds per m².
6. 150 000; i.e., five batches of 30 000.
7. If the birds roosted on the nest boxes they would be soiled with droppings.
8. If pullets have a very short day when laying begins the day length can be increased over a long peirod.
9. Flint grit inside the gizzard crushes up the bird's food.
10. Heavy hybrids lay larger eggs; they also lay brown eggs which many people prefer to white eggs.
11. 73%.

Glossary

Abomasum Fourth or true stomach of a ruminant.
Ad lib Always on offer (food).
Altitude The height above sea level.
Amphibian A cold-blooded vertebrate that develops from a water-dwelling creature, breathing with gills, to a land dweller breathing air.
Anaemic A blood condition where the ability of the blood to carry oxygen is reduced.
Anemometer Instrument that measures wind speed.
Annual A plant that completes one life cycle in one growing season.
Anterior Head end of animal.
Anther The part of a stamen that produces pollen.
Aorta Main artery.
Aphid A family of insects that live by sucking plant juice.
Arable Cultivated land.
Arboreal Tree living.
Artery Blood vessel taking blood from the heart.
Artificial insemination Manual introduction of viable sperm to uterus.
Auxanometer Instrument to measure increase in plant height.
Ascaris Internal parasite of pig.
Atrium Chamber in heart that receives blood from the veins.
Auricle Small extension of grass leaf blade.
Auxin Growth-regulating chemical produced in plants.
Awn Spike on the seeds of some grasses, e.g., barley.

Bacteria Extremely small life forms.
Bastard trenching A method of cultivating the soil to a depth of two spits.
Battery Cages Block of cages for housing laying birds.
Beaumont period A period of weather that favours potato blight.
Bedding plant Plant grown to plant into a flower border for one season's colour.
Biennial A plant that requires two growing seasons to complete its life cycle.
Bile Secretions of the liver.
Biological control The use of one organism to control another.
Bird A warm-blooded vertebrate covered with feathers.
Blanch Kept white by excluding light (vegetable).
Boar An entire male pig.
Bolus A pellet of food of a size that may be swallowed.
Brashing-up The removal of the lower branches of conifers.
Brassica A plant family – containing cabbage, turnip, etc.
British saddleback A breed of pig.
Broadcasting Sowing seeds by scattering them upon the surface.
Broilers Table chickens reared for killing at an early age (10–14 weeks).
Brood chamber A box of frames in a beehive in which the queen lays eggs and young are reared.
Brooder Equipment for keeping chicks warm.
Broody hen Hen in condition to incubate eggs and rear chicks.

Browsing The eating of leaves, shoots, etc., from the tops and side branches of trees and other large vegetation.

Buck Male rabbit or deer.

Bud A compact cluster of tiny leaves (or flowers) on a very small stem.

Budding A method of changing the variety of a tree or bush.

Bulb Roughly spherical plant structure having a reproductive and overwintering function, consists of layers of swollen leaves on a very short stem – e.g., onion.

Bulk tank A refrigerated tank which holds a day's milk production on the farm until it is collected.

Caecum Part of the gut of birds and some other animals.

Caesarean section Birth by cutting baby from mother's uterus with scalpel or similar instrument.

Calcareous soil A soil which contains a high proportion of calcium carbonate (lime).

Calcium carbonate Chemical substance from which egg shells are formed.

Calcicole Plant that requires alkaline soil.

Calcifuge Plant that grows well in acid soil.

Calomel A fungicide.

Calyx A ring of sepals on a flower or fruit.

Cambium A layer of dividing cells which lies between the xylem and phloem.

Candling Looking into eggs by means of a bright light.

Canine A tooth for flesh tearing – large in carnivores – often absent in herbivores.

Canopy The area covered by the spread of a tree's branches.

Capillary Very fine tube.

Carbohydrate Organic compound containing only carbon, hydrogen and oxygen (sugars and starch).

Cardinal points The points of a compass N, S, E and W.

Carnivore An animal that lives by eating other animals.

Castrate To remove the testicles.

Cattle Oxen which belong to the genus *Bos*.

Canker A fungus disease of bark.

Caudal disc Area around base of tail.

Cell Small mass of living material surrounded by a membrane. In plants also surrounded by a cellulose wall.

Cellulose Substance that gives strength to plant tissues.

Certified (stock or seed) Plants or tubers verified free from disease by a government body.

Cervix Passage between vagina and uterus.

Chalaza Twisted, thickened area in egg white which holds the yolk in position.

Chlorophyll The green pigment in plants which enables photosynthesis to take place.

Clamp An outside store of vegetables.

Clone Plants with identical genetic material, (i.e. propagated vegetatively from a single parent plant).

Clutch One sitting of eggs.

Coccidiosis A disease of rabbits and birds.

Cocoon Protective covering in which eggs or larvae or pupae develop.

Codling moth Insect pest of apples.

Colon Part of the large intestine.

Colostrum The first fluid produced by mammary glands of mammal after giving birth.

Compost 1. Decaying organic matter. 2. Material for filling seed boxes and plant pots.

Concentrates Foodstuffs with a high food value in a small bulk.

Conifer Trees that bear cones (yew and juniper have berries, and are also conifers).

Contractile roots Strong roots on some corms and tap roots that contract and pull the plant deeper into the soil.

Coprophagous pellets Special droppings produced by rabbits at night which are immediately ingested.

Cordon Fruit tree pruned to grow on a single stem.

Corm Underground swollen base of stem; stores food and produces new shoots from its buds.

Corolla The complete whorl of petals on a flower.

Cortex Tissue between vascular tissue and epidermis.

Cotyledon (a) The part of a seed in which food is stored; (b) The first leaf(s) produced by a seed.

Crankshaft A rod with right angle bends for converting up and down motion to revolving motion.
Creep Area available to young but not parents.
Crop Storage organ in bird for undigested food.
Cross-pollination Pollination of a flower with pollen from another flower.
Crown The uppermost parts of a tree.
Crown board Cover on top of a beehive to prevent bees entering the roof space.
Cull Inferior animal removed from herd or flock.
Culm Flower stalk of grass.
Cutting Part of a plant which has been cut off to grow a new plant.

Damping down Wetting floor and staging in a greenhouse.
Damping off Fungus disease of seedlings.
Deciduous Tree or shrub that bears no leaves in winter.
Deep litter Method of housing poultry or pigs.
Derris dust An insecticide manufactured from the root of the derris plant.
Dewlap Fold of loose skin hanging from the neck of cattle.
Diameter The distance across a circle, measured through centre.
Diaphragm Sheet of muscle dividing lung cavity from abdominal cavity.
Dicotyledon A class of plants.
Disbud Remove lateral buds.
Doe Female rabbit.
Dormant Alive but not growing or changing in any way.
Dorsal Back part of an animal.
Double digging A method of digging the soil to a depth of two spits.
Down Small fluffy feathers growing underneath the main feathers on ducks and geese.
Drake A male duck.
Drey The nest of a squirrel.
Drill A shallow trench drawn in the soil tilth in which seeds are sown.
Drupe Succulent fruit that contains a single seed.
Duodenum The part of the intestines nearest to an animal's stomach.

Edible Fit to be eaten.
Egg tooth Hard tip on bird's beak used to break out from the shell.
Embryo Baby plant or animal inside seed, egg or parent.
Encarsia formosa Insect parasite of whitefly.
Endodermis Innermost layer of cortex.
Entire Not castrated.
Enzootic pneumonia Disease of pig.
Enzyme A substance in animals which causes chemical changes to take place.
Ephemeral Short lived.
Epidermis Outermost layer of cells – one cell thick in plants, several cells thick in animals.
Epididymis Coiled duct attached to testis.
Erode Removal of top soil by natural forces.
Espallier Fruit trained with tiers of horizontal branches in one vertical plane.
Etiolated Plant growth with long internodes due to insufficient light.
Ewe Female sheep.

Faeces Undigested material passed from an animal's gut.
Fallopian tube Duct from ovary to horn of uterus.
Farrow Give birth (pig).
Fatty acid Chemical produced when fat is digested.
Fawn Young deer.
Feathered maiden Unpruned fruit tree two years old.
Ferret Half-tame variety of pole-cat, kept for driving rabbits from burrows.
Fertilisation The fusing of pollen and ovule, or sperm and ova.
Fertiliser Chemical material, rich in one or more plant nutrient.
Fibrous (a) Consisting of many fibres (e.g., peat; (b) Fibrous root – slender root, often with slender branches.
Field capacity The maximum amount of water that a fully drained soil can retain.
Filament The part of a stamen that holds the another.
Fish A cold-blooded vertebrate covered in scales, confined to an aquatic environment.
Flocculation Numbers of clay particles sticking together to form crumbs.

Floribunda Rose – that produces a number of open flowers on a single stem.

Flower The sexually reproductive part of a plant.

Flushing Feeding ewes extra food before mating.

Footrot Bacterial disease of sheep which causes lameness.

Formaldehyde Chemical substance used to sterilise soil.

Freeze branding Method of branding cattle by applying a very cold brand to the hide.

Frog hopper Insect pest of roses.

Fruit The fertilised ovary of a flower containing seeds.

Function Purpose.

Fungicide Chemical substance that kills fungi.

Gall bladder A sac, situated on the liver, in which bile collects.

Gamma-BHC An insecticide.

Gammexane An insecticide.

Gander Male goose.

Gastric juice Fluid produced inside the stomach by glands in the wall.

Geotropism The response to gravity by part of a plant.

Germination The breaking of dormancy by the embryo in a seed.

Gestation period The length of pregnancy.

Gilt Young female pig.

Gizzard The part of a bird's stomach that crushes the food.

Glume Protective layer around the flowers in a spikelet of grass.

Gosling Baby goose.

Grafting Method of changing the variety of a fruit tree.

Graminae Grass family.

Grazing The eating of grass, or other vegetation, from the ground.

Greenhouse Totally enclosed plant-growing structure of transparent material in which the grower can walk.

Harden off Acclimatise plants to outside conditions.

Haulm The leaves and stem of potatoes.

Hay Sun-dried grass.

Hectare Area equal to 10 000 m^2 (square with 100 m side).

Heifer Female cow before she has had her second calf.

Herbaceous plant Soft-stemmed plant – as distinct from trees and shrubs.

Herbicide Chemical substance that kills plants.

Herbivore An animal that lives by eating plants.

Hermaphrodite Individual plant or animal that has both male and female organs.

Hexagon Six-sided figure.

Hibernation An extended period of sleep during the winter months when food is not available.

Humidity The amount of water vapour in the air.

Humus Organic material in the final stages of decay.

Husk Parasitic disease of the lungs in cattle.

Hybrid Animal or plant produced by crossing two separate pure breeds.

Hydraulic Movement of liquids through pipes to give motive power.

Hydroponics Growing plants without soil in a nutrient solution.

Hypocotyl The length of 'stem' between the root and seed leaves of a seedling.

Incisor A tooth at the front of the jaw for biting.

Incubator Apparatus designed to keep eggs at constant temperature and humidity until the young hatch from them.

Indigenous Native (plant or animal).

Inflorescence Flowering shoot containing many individual flowers or groups of flowers.

Ingest Eat.

Inorganic Substance that has never lived.

Insect An invertebrate with three body parts and six jointed legs attached to the middle part.

Insecticide Chemical substance that kills insects.

Insectivore An animal that lives by eating insects and other invertebrates.

Insulator Material that will not conduct electricity.

Internode The part of the stem between one node and the next.

Intestine The part of an animal's digestive system where food passes into the blood-stream.

Invertebrate An animal without a backbone.
Irrigate Water plants.

John Innes compost Mixture of loam, coarse sand, peat and fertiliser, for growing plants in pots and boxes.

Kelp Burnt seaweed – rich in potash.
Kidney Animal organ that filters waste products from the blood.
Kilowatt A unit of power.

Lactation Period of milk secretion.
Lamb 1. Baby sheep. 2. The meat of a young sheep.
Landrace A breed of pig.
Larva (plural *larvae*) The feeding stage between egg and pupa in the life cycle of invertebrates. A larva usually looks very different from the adult form.
Latent heat Heat required by a substance to change from solid to liquid or liquid to gas.
Layering Method of propagation.
Leach The removal of soil salts in the drainage water.
Leaf miner Insect pest of chrysanthemums.
Leatherjacket Larva of crane fly (daddy long legs).
Leguminosae A plant family – peas, beans, clover, etc.
Lemma Part of the case that protects the sexual organs in a grass flower.
Ley A crop of grass or grass and clover mixture sown to last a limited number of years (1, 2, 3 or 4).
Ligament Band of strong tissue attached to bone.
Ligule Small transparent vertical projection on a grass sheath where leaf blade commences.
Litter The young produced by a single birth.
Liver Animal organ that stores food and produces bile.
Liver fluke Parasite of sheep and cattle affecting the liver.
Loam A soil formed from a mixture of sand, silt and clay particles.
Lodicule Very small part of a grass flower.
Lux Unit of light intensity.

Macro-organisms Living things large enough to be seen with the naked eye.
Maiden One year old fruit tree.
Malathion An insecticide.
Mammal A warm-blooded vertebrate that suckles its young.
Mastitis A disease of the udder in cattle.
MCPA A selective herbicide.
Medullary rays Food storage cells in wood.
Membrane A single layer of skin.
Meniscus The curved surface where liquid ends and air begins in a part filled tube.
Metabolism Chemical processes within an organism.
Micro-organisms Living things too small to be seen with the naked eye.
Micrometer screw gauge An instrument for accurately measuring the thickness of materials that are too thin to be measured with a ruler.
Micropyle Tiny hole in the testa of a seed.
Milking parlour Place where cattle are milked.
Mineral salts Inorganic chemical substances.
Molar A grinding tooth, situated at the back of the jaw.
Mole plough Plough that makes drainage tunnels in soil below the depth of normal cultivation.
Monocotyledon A class of plants.
Mulch A layer of decaying organic matter on the soil surface.
Mutton Meat from a sheep over 2 years old.

Nectar Sweet watery substance produced by flowers to attract insects.
Nematode Unsegmented worm.
Newton Unit of force.
Nitrogen An element which exists as gas in the air. An essential part of a protein molecule. An essential plant nutrient.
Node The place on a stem where the leaf stalk is attached.
Nodule Swelling on the root of leguminous plants which contains nutrifying bacteria.
Nursery Area where young plants or trees are raised.
Nymph A young insect that, except for size, resembles its parent.

Oesophagus Tube connecting mouth to stomach.
Oestrus The period during which a female will allow the male to mate.
Omasum The third 'stomach' of a ruminant.
Omnivore An animal that has a mixed diet (part plant and part animal), e.g., man.
Osmosis The movement of water through a semi-permeable membrane which is dividing two solutions of different concentrations.
Organ Part of an animal or plant that performs a special function, e.g., leaf or lungs.
Organic Substance that is living or has lived.
Ovary (Animal) The organ in the female that produces ova (eggs).
Ovary (Plant) The part of a flower that develops into a fruit.
Ovule The part of a flower that develops into a seed.

Palae Part of the case that protects the sexual organs in the grass flower.
Palisade layer Tissue in a plant leaf where most photosynthesis takes place.
Pallets Squares of wood upon which loads are stacked for transport.
Palpation Pregnancy test of rabbit by handling.
Pancreas Organ in animal that produces enzymes.
Paraquat A poisonous chemical substance which destroys chlorophyll.
Parasite Organism that obtains its food by living on or in another organism (its host).
Parenchyma Loosely-packed thin walled cells.
Ped Crumb of soil.
Pedigree An animal which is registered in the herd book of a breed society.
Penis Male reproductive and urinary organ.
Perennation The survival of a plant from year to year.
Perennial A plant that flowers each year.
Pesticide Chemical poisonous to pests.
Petal One of the parts of a flower – often brightly coloured.
Petiole The leaf stalk.
Photoperiodism Response of plants to changing day length.

Phototropism The response to light by part of a plant.
pH The scale by which the degree of acidity is measured.
Pituitary Gland situated under the brain.
Phloem Tissue in plants which transports sugars and other organic material.
Phosphate A chemical element essential to plants and animals.
Ploche Circular cloche.
Plumule Small shoot inside, or just emerging from, a seed.
Poach The destruction of soil structure by treading.
Pollard A shape of tree produced by regular lopping of branches from the trunk.
Pollen The male sex cells produced by a flower.
Pollination The transfer of pollen to the stigma of a flower.
Porter bee escape Metal appliance which allows bees to pass from one section of the hive to another, but not to return.
Posterior Tail end of animal.
Potash A chemical element essential to plants and animals.
Potometer An instrument to measure transpiration rate.
Poult Baby turkey.
Preen gland Oil-producing gland on a bird's back, just forward from the tail.
Pregnant Refers to female that has young developing inside her uterus.
Prevailing wind The most frequent wind direction.
Prick out Plant out seedlings to allow more space for growth.
Progeny Offspring.
Propagation Increasing the numbers of plants from seeds or parent stock.
Propane Inflammable gas usually supplied in a pressurised metal cylinder.
Propolis Sticky yellow substance collected by bees.
Prostate Male gland of mammals producing substances to add to sperms.
Protein An organic compound that contains the element nitrogen.
Protozoa One celled animals.

Protoplasm Living material in a plant or animal cell.
Proventriculus The enzyme-producing part of bird's stomach.
Prune Cut shoots from a plant (usually a tree or shrub).
Pullet Female hen under 18 months old.
Pulpy kidney Disease of sheep.
Pupa The non-feeding developmental stage between larva and adult of many invertebrates.

Queen excluder Sheet of metal punched with holes, large enough for worker bees to pass through but too small to allow queens or drones to pass through.

Rabies Fatal disease of mammals.
Raddle Coloured chalk-like substance.
Radicle Small root inside, or just emerging from a seed.
Ram Entire male sheep.
Raffia Fibre from palm leaves used to tie up plants.
Receptacle Top of a flower stalk.
Rectum Last part of large intestine.
Red spider mite Minute pest of greenhouse plants and fruit trees.
Reptile A cold-blooded air breathing vertebrate, covered in scales, which reproduces by laying eggs on land.
Respiration Breathing (animal). Obtaining energy from sugar and oxygen (plant).
Resazurin test Method of testing the keeping quality of milk.
Residual herbicide Plant killing substance which persists in the soil.
Reticulum Second 'stomach' of a ruminant.
Reversion Virus disease of black currant.
Rhizome Underground stem (usually horizontal).
Ringworm Fungus disease of cattle.
Rodent Gnawing mammal with continually growing incisors.
Rooting powder Synthetic auxin-like material which speeds the rooting of cuttings.
Rootstock Base upon which grafts or buds are grown.
Roughage Fibrous food (e.g., hay).

Rumen First 'stomach' of a ruminant.
Ruminant An animal which chews the cud.

Salmonella Micro-organism that causes food poisoning.
Sawfly An insect pest of apples.
Scour Excessive looseness of the bowels.
Scrotum Sac that contains the testicles.
Secateur Cutting tool used for pruning tress and bushes.
Seed A tiny dormant plant with a store of food surrounded by a protective coat.
Selective herbicide A chemical substance which kills weeds and leaves the crop unharmed.
Self-fertile A flower that sets with its own pollen.
Self-pollination Pollination of a flower with its own pollen.
Semen Sperm-charged fluid produced by male.
Seminal vesicle Male organ which stores sperm.
Semi-permeable membrane Membrane which allows passage of water but not dissolved substances.
Sepal The outermost, leaf-like structure of a flower.
Shrub A moderate size woody perennial with many branches at the base.
Sigmoid 'S'-shaped.
Silage Partially decayed, stored grass.
Silt Mineral particles, larger than clay and smaller than fine sand.
Simazine Residual herbicide.
Sink Wedge-shaped cut in a tree made as first part of the felling operation.
Slurry Very wet dung and mud.
Smoker Beekeepers' appliance for puffing smoke.
Sodium chlorate A chemical substance toxic to plants.
Soft fruit Fruit grown on shrubs, canes and herbaceous plants.
Solenoid Coil of wire which becomes magnetic when conducting electricity.
Sow Mother pig.
Spikelet A cluster of individual flowers in a grass plant.
Spongy tissue Tissue in a leaf which allows movement of air.
Spit The length of the blade of a spade.

Spline Rectangular key fitting into grooves in a shaft.
Stamen The male part of a flower.
Starch Insoluble carbohydrate.
Steaming up Feeding a mammal extra food before giving birth to increase subsequent milk yield.
Sterile Unable to breed.
Sterilise To kill all micro-organisms within or attached to a substance or article.
Stigma The female part of a flower that receives pollen.
Stimulus A change in the external environment of plant or animal which produces a response in that plant or animal.
Stolon Horizontal stem that grows above the ground along the soil surface.
Stool The roots and lower stem of a perennial.
Straw Dead leaves and stems of cereal crops left after the grain has been removed.
Strike Disorder of sheep caused by the greenbottle fly.
Stoma (plural *stomata*) Tiny pore on the surface of leaf.
Stubble Stems of plants remaining above the soil after the top parts have been harvested.
Style The part of a flower between the stigma and the ovary.
Sub-clinical Without visible effect (disease).
Subsoil The layer of lighter coloured material directly underneath the topsoil.
Super Box of shallow frames in which bees store honey.
Symbiosis An association between two organisms from which both derive benefit.
Syrup A strong solution of sugar in water for feeding to bees.
Systemic Capable of moving through the systems and tissues of a plant or animal.

Tap-root A single main root that grows vertically downwards.
Teat Nipple through which milk passes from the mammary gland.
Tendril A slender outgrowth from a plant that curls around objects to give the plant support.
Terminal bud The bud on the tip of a branch or shoot.

Testa Seed coat.
Testis Organ in male which produces sperm.
Thigmotropism The response to touch by part of a plant.
Thinning The removal of some plants or trees to allow more space for the ones remaining to grow.
Thorax 1. Insects – the body part, behind the head to which the legs are attached.
2. Vertebrates – region of body that contains heart and lungs.
Tiller Bud of a grass plant.
Tilth The fineness of the structure of the surface soil.
Tonne 1000 kilograms.
Top fruit Fruit which grows upon trees.
Trachea Windpipe.
Transformer A device that reduces the voltage of an electric current.
Translocation Movement of chemical substance within a plant.
Transpiration Passage of water from soil to air through a plant.
Trichlorphon An insecticide.
Tropism A plant's response to a stimulus.
Truss Single bunch of tomatoes attached to the plant.
Tuber Part of a root or stem swollen with food stores.
Tuberculosis (T.B.) An animal disease, usually infecting the lungs.
Tup Entire male sheep.
Turgor Cell wall of plant kept rigid by high water content of the vacuole.

Udder Milk glands of cow, sheep, etc.
Ultra violet Invisible solar radiation with wave length a little shorter than violet.
Umbelliferae Plant family which includes parsnip, parsley and carrot.
Ureter Duct from kidney to bladder.
Uterus Female organ in which young develop.

Vagina Duct of female that receives penis during mating.
Variety A strain of plants within a species that have similar special characteristics.

Vascular bundle Group of vessels in plant which includes xylem and phloem.
Vein Blood vessel taking blood towards the heart.
Vena cava Main vein.
Vent The outlet in the back of a bird through which faeces and eggs pass.
Ventral Underneath part of animal.
Ventricle Chamber of heart that forces blood into arteries by contraction.
Vermin Animals which damage crops or stored food.
Vernalisation A change in plant behaviour induced by abnormal temperature.
Vertebrate An animal with a backbone.
Viable Having the ability of germinate (seeds).
Villus Finger-like projection on inside wall of intestine.
Virus Extremely small form of life, that can live only in other living things.
Vitamins Chemical substances essential to animal health.
'Vitax' Chemical additive for composts which contains all the essential plant nutrients.
Vixen Female fox.
Vulva Exterior part of the female organ.

Warble-fly Insect parasite of cattle.
Warfarin Poison used against rodents.
Wean The removal of the baby animals from their mother as they are old enough to take adult food.
Weed A plant growing where it is not wanted.
Whitefly Sucking insect pest of greenhouse plants.
Winter moth Insect pest of fruit trees.

Xylem Tubular tissue which conducts water up plants and gives support.

Index

Acaricide, 60
Apples, 71
  aphid, 92
  grafting, 73
  pests and diseases, 79–81
  pollination, 76
  rootstocks, 72
  storing, 77
  tree shapes, 74–75
  varieties, 76
Artificial insemination, 120–121
Auxanometer, 15, 16

Bacteria
  de-nitrifying, 23
  in milk, 131–132
  in rumen, 108
  rhizobium, 23
  soil, 41
Battery cages, 145–146
Bedding plants, 43
Biological control, 59–60
Black spot, 92
Blackcurrant, 68–70
Broilers, 141–144
Butter, 115–116

Calf rearing, 130–131
Cambium, 9
Carbon cycle, 24–25
Carbon dioxide, 16–18, 21, 25
Cattle, 114
  artificial insemination, 120
  beef production, 134
  breeds, 116–119
  dentition, 134
  embryo transplants, 121
  feeding, 128–130
  gestation, 134
  grading up, 122
  housing, 124–126
  husk, 136
  life cycle, 133

  mastitis, 132
  milk fever, 139
  milk let-down, 135
  milk records, 123
  oestrus, 134
  production rations, 129
  ringworm, 136
  teeth, 135
  warble fly, 137
Cheese, 116
Chemicals, 32
Chlorophyll, 16
Chrysanthemum, 83
  cuttings, 84
  disbudding, 85
  eel worm, 88
  later flowering, 86
  leaf miner, 86–87
  photoperiodism, 86
  stools, 83
  stopping, 84
  support, 85
Cloches, 33–35
Codling moth, 79–81
Compost, 41–46
  John Innes, 43
  no soil, 43
Controlled environment, 141–142
Cordon, 75
Cortex, 8
Creep grazing, 104
Cucumber (*Cucumis sativus*), 56
Cuticle, 12

Damping off, 58
Deep litter, 146–147
Dehorning, 136
Direct drilling, 29
Disbudding, 85

Egg,
  breeds, 149
  feeding, 148
  lighting, 147–148

  production, 145–150
Embryo transplanting, 121
Encarsia formosa, 59
Endodermis, 8, 14
Epidermis, 8, 9, 14
Espallier, 75

Feeding, beef cattle, 134
  broilers, 144
  chickens, 148
  dairy cattle, 128
  sheep, 103
  turkeys, 153
Fertiliser, 13, 21–22
Flowers, 83–92
Footrot, 109
Formaldehyde, 41
Free range, 147
Freeze branding, 128
Froghopper, 92

Garden design, 92–97
Garden frames, 33, 35–36
Glucose, 25
Grafting, 73–74
Grass, 80, 94–95
Greenhouse, 33
  effect, 33
  fumigation, 59
  fungus diseases, 60
  heating, 39
  lean-to, 39
  materials, 37
  mobile, 38
  multiple span, 37
  red spider mite, 59
  site, 37
  three-quarter span, 39
  ventilation, 37, 49
  watering, 46, 49
  whitefly, 58
Grow-bags, 50

Hardening off, 36
Health and Safety at Work Act, 32
Herbicide, contact, 28
    residual, 28
    selective, 27
    translocated, 28
Herd book, 121–122
Houseplants, 51, 52
Husk, 136–137
Hydroponics, 51

John Innes base, 42
    composts, 42, 43

Lawns, 94–95
Leaf, area index, 19, 20
    internal structure, 12
    miner, 86–87
    orientation, 20
    shape, 20
    variegated, 18
Liver fluke, 111–112
Loam, 41, 42

Mastitis, 132
MCPA, 29
Micropropagation, 57
Milk, composition, 115
    fever, 139
    let-down, 135
    machines, 127–128
    parlours, 125
    recording, 123
    secretion, 135–136
Mineral salts, 14
Mist propagation, 53–54
Mulching, 66

Nematodes, 64
Nitrogen, 21, 22
    cycle, 23–24
Noise, 32
Nutrient film technique, 51

Osmosis, 13, 14
Outwintering, 124

Palisade tissue, 12
Paraquat, 28–29

Parenchyma, 9
Peat, 42
Peck order, 144–145
Pedigree, 121–124
Pepper, 56
Petiole, 12
Pheromone trap, 83
Phloem, 8
Phosphate, 21, 22
Photoperiodism, 86
Photosynthesis, 16–19
Plant growth, 15–16
Plant nutrients, 21
Polythene tunnel, 38
Ponds, 96
Potash, 21, 22
Potometer, 14, 15
Potting on, 48
Potting up, 47
Poultry drinker, 151
Pre-emergent spraying, 29
Pricking out, 45
Progeny testing, 121
Propagation, air layering, 55
    budding, 90
    hardwood cutting, 69
    rootstocks, 72
    steam cuttings, 83–84
Propagator, 39, 40
Pruning, apple, 74–76
    blackcurrant, 69
    cuts, 70
    raspberry, 67
Pulpy kidney, 109

Rare breeds, 120
Raspberry, 65–67
Red spider mite, 59–60
Resazurin test, 131
Respiration (plant), 21
Reversion, 70
Ring culture, 50
Ringworm, 136
Rockeries, 95–96
Root hair, 8, 14
Rose, aphid, 92
    budding, 90
    bud treatment, 91
    frog hopper, 92
    fungus diseases, 92
    growing, 91
    rootstocks, 89
    types, 88–89
Ruminant digestion, 107

Sand, 42
Scion, 73, 74, 90
Seed sowing 44
Semen, 120
Sheep, breeds, 99–100
    digestion, 107
    dipping, 102
    dog, 106
    feeding, 103
    foot rot, 109
    housing, 101
    products 81
    scab, 109–110
    strike, 110
    wool, 98–99
Simazine, 30
Sodium chlorate, 27
Soil, sterilisation, 40, 41, 51
    warming, 40
    water 14
Spindle bush, 75
Spongy tissue, 12
Spraying, 30–31, 67
Starch, 17, 19
Stoma, 10, 14
Stopping (a plant), 84
Strawberry, 62–65
Strike, 110–111
Sulphuric acid, 27
Sweet pepper, 56
Systemic insecticide, 92

Tissue culture, 57
Tomato, 46–50
Trace elements, 21
Translocation, 16
Transpiration, 14–15
Turgor pressure, 7, 11
Turkeys, 150–151

Vascular bundle, 9

Warble fly, 137–138
White fly, 58–59
Winter moth, 78–79

Xylem, 8, 14